MASTERS OF PAINTING

MASTERS OF PAINTING

THEIR WORKS / THEIR LIVES / THEIR TIMES

BERNARDINE KIELTY

DOUBLEDAY & COMPANY, INC. / GARDEN CITY, NEW YORK

A.C.L. ART REFERENCE BUREAU: *Pages 76, 77, 85, 88.*

AGRACI ART REFERENCE BUREAU: *Pages 41 (bottom), 51 (top), 75 (bottom), 145, 169.*

ALINARI ART REFERENCE BUREAU: *Pages 16 (bottom), 19, 20, 27 (bottom, right), 28 (bottom), 29, 33, 36, 39 (top), 40, 42 (top), 44 (top), 45 (bottom), 46, 48, 49, 52 (bottom), 53, 54, 55 (bottom), 56, 57, 58 (center), 60, 62, 65 (left), 66, 68, 69, 71 (top), 72, 73, 75 (top), 89 (bottom), 92, 96 (bottom), 104 (top, right), 108 (bottom), 119 (right), 126 (top), 136, 181.*

AMERICAN HERITAGE: *Pages 42 (bottom), 47 (bottom).*

ANDERSON ART REFERENCE BUREAU: *Pages 17, 21, 25, 27 (bottom, left), 41 (top), 45 (top), 51 (bottom), 52 (top), 58 (left and right), 64, 65 (right), 68 (top), 71 (bottom), 80, 90, 95 (bottom), 111, 116, 117, 119, (left), 121 (bottom), 123.*

ART REFERENCE BUREAU: *Pages 23, 26, 31, 34 (bottom), 35, 39 (bottom), 55 (top), 59, 78 (bottom), 82 (top), 83, 97, 101 (left), 106, 118, 129, 138.*

BROGI ART REFERENCE BUREAU: *Pages 18, 22, 27 (top), 28 (top).*

BRUCKMANN ART REFERENCE BUREAU: *Pages 81, 82 (bottom), 84, 104 (bottom).*

BULLOZ ART REFERENCE BUREAU: *Page 154.*

CAMERA CLIX: *Page 148.*

CLOWES FUND COLLECTION, INDIANAPOLIS: *Page 100.*

COPYRIGHT, THE FRICK COLLECTION, 1936: *Page 105.*

COURTAULD INSTITUTE—ART REFERENCE BUREAU: *Page 165.*

COURTESY OF THE NEW YORK HISTORICAL SOCIETY, NEW YORK: *Page 47 (top).*

FOGG ART MUSEUM, HARVARD UNIVERSITY, CAMBRIDGE, GRENVILLE L. WINTHROP COLLECTION: *Page 139 (bottom).*

GIRAUDON: *Pages 15, 66, 67, 79 (top), 86, 87, 110, 126 (bottom), 158, 162, 163.*

HISPANIC SOCIETY OF AMERICA: *Page 121 (top).*

JOHN FREEMAN: *Pages 11, 14, 50, 78 (top), 98, 127, 131.*

MARBURG ART REFERENCE BUREAU: *Pages 12, 91 (top, left), 93, 96 (top), 101 (right), 103 (bottom), 107, 108 (top).*

MUSEUM OF FINE ARTS, BOSTON: *Page 130 (top).*

NATIONAL GALLERY ART REFERENCE BUREAU: *Pages 128, 130 (bottom), 132, 134.*

NATIONAL PORTRAIT GALLERY, ART REFERENCE BUREAU: *Page 97.*

PHOTO BRUSSELLE: *Page 79 (bottom).*

PHOTO FROM EUROPEAN: *Page 16 (top).*

PHOTOGRAPH BY ERIC POLLITZER: *Pages 115, 122, 143, 151, 171, 175.*

PHOTOGRAPH BY MEYER ERWIN: *Page 103 (top).*

SCALA: *Pages 34 (top), 38, 70.*

THREE LIONS: *Page 150 (bottom).*

The painting on the title page is *Christ at the Sea of Galilee* by Tintoretto. Samuel H. Kress Collection, National Gallery of Art, Washington, D.C.

The author and Doubleday & Company, Inc., have taken all possible care to trace the ownership of every work of art included in this book and to make full acknowledgment for its use. If any errors have accidentally occurred they will be corrected in subsequent editions, provided notification is sent to the publisher.

LIBRARY OF CONGRESS CATALOG CARD NUMBER 63–15118

COPYRIGHT © 1964 BY BERNARDINE KIELTY SCHERMAN

ALL RIGHTS RESERVED

LITHOGRAPHED IN THE UNITED STATES OF AMERICA

FOREWORD

To appreciate and comprehend a painting, it is necessary not only to look at it with attention, but to have some familiarity with its place in the history of art. A painting, after all, is not merely the product of its creator's imagination and skill. Painters throughout history have been influenced by earlier painters, as well as by the religious, political, economic, scientific and social events of their times.

This book covers the artists whose works are landmarks in the history of painting. It is a short illustrated survey of a long story, beginning in the fourteenth century with Giotto and ending with Cézanne in the late nineteenth century. It includes descriptive records of the important periods during which these men have worked, biographical accounts of the artists themselves, and reproductions of many of their famous paintings. It is designed to act as a stimulant for those to whom the enjoyment and study of pictures is a brand new experience; and to enhance the pleasure and satisfy the curiosity of those who already have a casual acquaintance with art.

For the reader whose appetite for seeing pictures may thus have been whetted, a list of American museums and galleries where works by the painters mentioned in these pages may be found is included at the back of the book.

Bernardine Kielty

CONTENTS

MASTERS OF PAINTING

BYZANTINE SCHOOL. Madonna and Child
Enthroned. Mellon Collection, National
Gallery of Art, Washington, D.C.

A Thousand Years Went By ...

Picture painting did not begin on a certain day in a certain year
in a certain century. Long before this story opens, prehistoric
man had made pictures on the walls of his cave. Primitive tribes
had painted totem poles. The ancient Egyptians pictured kings
and queens and slaves in their tombs, and the highly civilized
Greeks and Romans adorned the walls of their homes and tem-
ples with paintings. Art flourished in distant Asia.

This story of painting, however, starts with the Italian Renaissance, which in many ways marked the beginning of the modern
world. It concerns the famous pictures we all may see in museums and galleries, and the artists who painted them—men who
had the wondrous gift of transferring what they saw in the
world about them onto canvas or wood or the plaster of walls.

A thousand years passed between the end of the Roman Empire and the sunburst that was the Italian Renaissance. It was a
long bleak space—a stretch of time almost beyond imagining.
But during those endless centuries there were gradual, slow-mov-
ing, at first almost imperceptible changes; and out of these changes
grew a bright new world.

ENGLISH MASTER. The Wilton Diptych,
National Gallery, London.

Cathedral Tympanum, Middle West
Door. Autun.

The first half of that thousand years is called the Dark Ages.
It is only a name, but one that has lasted. Roughly, the Dark
Ages covered the years from A.D. 475 when Attila the Hun sacked
Rome, to 1066 when William the Norman conquered Britain.
About that long passage of time the history of Europe has very
little to record: we know that barbarian tribes from the north and
east, from the plains of Asia and Hungary, rode their wild destruc-
tive way across Europe. They were the Goths, the Huns, the Van-
dals. They destroyed the city of Rome and overran the Roman
colonies in the regions north of the Alps. The people in villages
and towns fled before them. Cities were burned, inhabitants slaughtered, civilization was all but destroyed. Few roads were left, no
schools, no organization, no rulers. Grass grew between the cobbles
where proud charioteers once had driven. It is said that for one
short period the great city of imperial Rome was entirely abandoned: not a living creature remained but the rats. The Dark Ages
was a time of migration and constant bloodshed.

12

Only the Church remained steadfast.

A little candle of learning burned faintly through the long night. In the monasteries, in quiet isolated spots in Ireland and in France, monks whose names we can never know bent over sheets of vellum, and for the glory of God copied pages of the Bible. With finest brushes they painstakingly painted tiny, brilliant illustrations of the Bible stories, and made entrancing decorations in the margins of the pages. These we can see in old illuminated manuscripts like *The Book of Hours* (see page 15).

The monks did more than keep learning alive. The time came when the restless pagan tribesmen gradually settled down. They stopped their fighting, and for safety gathered in small groups, usually near the big sprawling monasteries. They saw the gardens that the monks cultivated, they heard the bells, they filtered, in time, into the monastery chapel. In this way, very gradually, the monks showed them the rudiments of civilization and converted them to Christianity. This was in the lands of Western Europe.

Christianity had also been kept alive at the eastern end of the Mediterranean Sea. In A.D. 330 the Roman Emperor Constantine had conquered and rebuilt the city of Byzantium (for centuries called Constantinople, and now Istanbul), and made it Christian. When Rome grew weak and lost her power, when the barbarians overrode Europe, the center of the Christian world shifted to Byzantium, the all-powerful city on the Sea of Bosporus. Magnificent churches were built, where vast congregations of the faithful gathered. High over their heads, painted on the enormous dome, the majestic figure of Christ gazed down upon them, His right hand raised in blessing; or the *Madonna and Child,* enthroned like an Empress, was painted in gleaming reds and blues against a curtain of gold (see page 10).

They were the symbols of an unchanging religion. Gigantic figures, erect, stiff, always looking straight ahead, always making the same gestures.

While the monk in his monastery in the forest was worshiping God through his beautiful, small, illuminated pages, the dazzling emperors of Byzantium worshiped Him by way of the walls and domes of their huge churches. Both had their influence on the painting that was to come.

It was during the eleventh and twelfth centuries—the last centuries of the Middle Ages—that East and West came face to face. Europe was still poor and backward, though the light of dawn had begun to glimmer, faint but slowly brightening. Constantinople remained the richest and the most powerful Christian city in the world. But the infidels of Asia were moving close around her. They had conquered the Holy Land and occupied Jerusalem. Now only a strip of water lay between them and the great city.

This was the situation that brought about the Crusades and started vast hordes of pilgrims on their incredibly long journey eastward. They went to fight for Christendom, in one of the longest drawn-out yet one of the most dramatic episodes in history.

The First Crusade was led by Peter the Hermit, a simple man who rode bareheaded and barefoot on a small donkey at the head of a straggling mass of sinners. They were outlaws, robbers, and murderers from the Western world, who by this holy journey hoped to have their sins forgiven.

But this was only a prelude. Nearly every year a new band of Crusaders started out for the Holy Land, led now by the barons, the princes, the saintly and not-so-saintly kings of France and England and Germany. Adventurers all, they made their way across and around Europe, by horse, by ship, and on foot. For over two hundred years Crusade after Crusade merged in one continuing movement from West to East and back again.

Thousands went forth, far fewer returned. But of those who did come back many had seen Byzantium. They had seen its treasures of gold, the stiff gigantic figures on the walls of its churches. Now when they straggled home, these knightly warriors yearned to show a new pathway to God in their own lands.

So it was, after the peak of the Crusades, that the great churches which we now know as Gothic cathedrals started to rise in France and England and Germany—Notre Dame and

14

ENGLISH MASTER. The Wilton Diptych (detail). National Gallery, London.

PAUL OF LIMBURG AND BROTHERS. August, from the Very Rich Book of Hours of the Duke of Berry. Condé Museum, Chantilly.

Chartres, Lincoln and Salisbury, Strasbourg, and Cologne. They were inspired by the returning crusaders but built by the common people. Each mighty structure took many years to build—sometimes several generations—and it was the people and their children and after that their grandchildren who lovingly carried the stones from the hillsides to the church and put them one above the other. Some of the men, handy with a chisel, carved the stone in heavenly figures. They had seen the illuminated manuscripts in the monasteries, and they now decorated their doorways and their altars with virgins of divine sweetness and innocent childlike saints, with dogs to bark off evil, and dragons to be overcome. The paintings were the same: mystical tender angels all alike, a gentle Virgin, and an aura of calm religious beauty as in *The Wilton Diptych* (page 11 and detail opposite)

The sun through the stained-glass windows glowed with rainbow colors. The tall slender spires, the pointed windows, the high-vaulted ceilings soared heavenward.

Such was the art of the Middle Ages, religious, mystical, saintly, and drenched with emotion.

The story of painting begins as the Middle Ages were merging into the Renaissance. It opens in Italy at the start of our own era, and moves without a break from Italy in the fourteenth century, through generation after generation of painters, to the present. The world and the people underwent tremendous upheavals, but art endured. Every great artist learned something from those who painted before him, he added the touch of his own vital personality, and helped forge one link of beauty in the magnificent chain that binds the art of early Italy with our own.

15

TWO VIEWS OF FLORENCE.

16

PART ONE
THE OLD MASTERS

★ ★ ★

Chapter 1

FLORENCE

Florence, birthplace of the Renaissance, is a beautiful city in Northern Italy, encircled with wooded hills. Winding through the city the Arno River flows in long graceful curves. The air is clear and bright.

During the fifteenth century Florence was a city on tiptoes. These were the 1400s, which the Italians call the *Quattrocento*. Her people were vigorous and eager. Rich and poor alike were people of lofty ideals, to whom learning meant more than money, and art was the breath of life. They looked upon poets and painters, sculptors and architects, as leaders. In the space of a hundred years more men of genius lived in Florence than anywhere else at any time in history, except in ancient Athens. With Athens and Rome and Jerusalem, Florence stands among the cities of all time that have had the deepest effect on the spirit of man.

Florence was already aglow with life in 1300, a small city entrenched within strong walls, surrounded by smiling fields and vineyards and olive orchards. Inside the walls it was exciting just to be alive. Men worked in their doorways in order not to miss what was going on in the streets. The market place was gay and noisy, with merchants, nobles, artisans, beggars, and gamblers, maids, musicians mingled together in a bright mass of color—far brighter than we see in our streets today.

Young men-about-town did not wear dull suits, all alike, in the Quattrocento, as they do now. Their legs were encased in long, tight-fitting bright-colored hose, purple or red or green, their tunics were of another color, and high caps of still another. Elderly gentlemen pursuing their business were well covered in rich brocaded capes. And the black notes of the students' garb, scattered here and there, only accented the brilliant spectacle.

The Florentines were filled with pride in their city. They commissioned an architect, as early as 1294, to build a cathedral of such splendor and beauty "that no human power could ever conceive its equal." Opposite the cathedral stood the octagonal Baptistry of St. John, where the people gathered to read stories of the Old Testament told in the magnificent sculptures of its bronze doors.

Palazzo Vecchio, Florence.

GHIBERTI. East Doors (the Doors of Paradise). Baptistry, Florence.

The nobles and the rich merchants lived in stone palaces along the narrow streets. These were no longer fortresses with dungeons and slits for windows, built for safety as they had been in medieval days. Nor were they ornate. Their heavy, gray stone exteriors were strong but not forbidding. The pattern of windows and entrances, the occasional balconies, the proportions were all designed to please the onlooker. While indoors, for the pleasure of the intimate family, everything was in the best of taste—furniture, vases, tapestries, enamels, majolica. Nothing was mediocre.

The people of Florence grew up surrounded by beauty.

They were free and independent. Florence was a rich city, and
wool was the backbone of her wealth. Imported from England,
the wool was woven in Florence into cloth and sold throughout
Italy and the rest of Europe. Three hundred wool weavers' ships
were running full tilt when business was at its height, and the
weavers' guild was the most powerful in the city. Guilds were
organizations similar to our labor unions, designed to maintain
the standards and protect the interests of various trades. Leather
workers had their guild, and the wood carvers, the goldsmiths,
the metalworkers, the barbers. These guilds were made up of
the "common people," who had only lately emerged from the
mists of the Middle Ages. They were no longer downtrodden
serfs, but citizens of a republic. Theirs was the voice of Florence.

Everyone was eager to work. In Florence idleness was despised. But the Florentines were not only incredibly energetic.
They were people of rare spirit. Dante, one of the greatest poets
of all time, was a Florentine, and alive to the changing times.
Unlike the poets before him he wrote his poetry in Italian,
the language spoken in the streets, instead of in Latin, which only
the educated could read. The famous storyteller Boccaccio and the
poet Petrarch both lived in Florence at the same time. St. Francis,

Attributed to GIOTTO. St. Francis Preaching to the Birds. Church of S. Francesco,
Assisi.

19

GIOVANNI BELLINI. Portrait of a Condottiere. Samuel H. Kress Collection, National Gallery of Art, Washington, D.C.

BRONZINO. Portrait of Cosimo I de' Medici. Pitti Palace, Florence.

though not a Florentine, came from not faraway, and was the most beloved saint. Like the people of Florence he enjoyed life and delighted not only in his fellow men but in animals and in all nature. He was humble, never proud. And this humility and directness and simplicity were dear to the hearts of the intelligent Florentines.

Although the masses of the people, through their guilds, were finding their voice, Florence, as well as the other Italian cities, had powerful rulers. A small number of influential families had grown up in the course of the years, descendants of successful soldiers (*condottieri*) or natural leaders or men of wealth. In some cities these rulers were despots of unbelievable cruelty. They exiled all rivals or paid assassins to do away with them—sometimes even within the family circle. Yet these tyrants were the patrons of art. In the Quattrocento the combination of democracy and tyranny on the whole worked out well.

The foremost family in Florence at this time was the Medici.

Cosimo de' Medici, father of the family, was a profoundly wise, practical, and learned man. He ruled Florence from 1434 to 1464, and in all that time it is said that no one was ill-treated. He was the "invisible" ruler, in that he never held office except for a brief six months. He was a merchant and banker with connections throughout Europe. As a man of sharp business sense he knew how to manage Florence's financial affairs, which was important. But of more lasting significance was his encouragement of art and learning. Unlike the rulers in other cities, he held no court. The palace he lived in was more modest than the palaces of many other well-to-do Florentines. He walked through the streets dressed like any other businessman, stopped to chat with friends, and was entirely at home in his lovely city. Painters and sculptors and architects were his companions.

While the other Italian states were at war with one another, Cosimo maintained peace. He built the first public library in Europe. He promoted the study of ancient culture and planned to establish the Platonic Academy (which his grandson did establish)—a meeting place where scholars and students could come together to read and to discuss the learning and philosophy of the Greeks.

Cosimo ruled Florence for thirty years, and after his death at the age of seventy-five, the proceeds of his huge banking business continued to be devoted to art and culture for three generations.

Piero de' Medici was Cosimo's son, and Lorenzo the Magnificent his grandson. All three were brilliant men and all of them were afflicted by an excruciatingly painful disease—a form of arthritis which kept Cosimo in constant pain throughout most of his long life, which killed Piero off at the age of fifty-three, and Lorenzo at forty-three, but in no way impaired their spirit. All three loved their city passionately. They were close to the people—far closer than rulers of any other day. On matters of beauty they saw eye to eye. The Medici stood behind the artists of Florence. They believed in them. They supported them when necessary.

And the pictures painted in the days of these three great men are now the glory of Italy and the world.

This period is known as the Early Renaissance. Renaissance means "rebirth." Ancient learning was indeed reborn. After the fall of Constantinople to the Turks in 1453 old Greek manuscripts found their way into Italy and were translated. The same year marked the invention of printing. Ancient statues were unearthed.

But along with interest in the old came a fresh new concern for the natural world. The Florentines were interested not in death but in life; not in heaven and hell, but in the earth. They were tired of smiling medieval angels and of the stiff gigantic figures of Byzantium. Their artists began to look at people's faces around them. They studied the human body with all the excitement of explorers in new lands. The Renaissance, more than a "rebirth," was a rediscovery of man and nature.

The "Man of the Renaissance" was a thinker, an artist, an investigator, man of learning, and man of action. He lived a dozen lives in one. His kind no longer exists.

Giotto

c. 1266–1337

Giotto was the white light that came before the dawn of the Renaissance. Without him this story of painting might have taken a far different course.

He was born Giotto di Bondone in the village of Colle, in a pretty valley about fourteen miles from Florence. His parents owned goats and sheep, and the story goes that one day while still a boy he was up on the mountainside tending the animals. But he was not dreaming the day away, or playing a pipe, as shepherds and goatherds are said to do. He was scratching the figure of an animal on a large flat stone.

A man passing by on his way over the hill looked down over the boy's shoulder and was amazed at the skillful drawing. The man was CIMABUE, a well-known painter of Florence, who at once asked the boy to come to his studio.

Whether or not the story is true, it is quite likely that Giotto did become an apprentice in Cimabue's workshop. It was the busiest one in Florence, and nowhere else could he have been launched as quickly as he was on a painting career. The interesting thing is that Cimabue was still painting in the well-known Byzantine way, and that Giotto was the first artist to break away from that tradition.

In those days there were no art schools. Artists were craftsmen like carpenters and goldsmiths. (In Florence the artists' guild belonged to the guild which included doctors and apothecaries.) They learned their trade by working in the studio of an established

CIMABUE. Madonna Enthroned. Uffizi Gallery, Florence.

GIOTTO. Dante, detail from fresco of Paradise. Bargello, Florence.

artist who took orders for altarpieces, frescoes, wedding chests, flags, banners. There were no tubes of ready-made paint, so the young apprentices ground colors for their masters. They cleaned brushes. After a time, when they had learned how to use a brush themselves, they helped by painting backgrounds under the master's direction, or areas of the high walls or ceilings that were hard to reach.

There were no museums and no exhibitions. An artist did not paint a picture in the vague hope that someone would buy it, as artists do now. He waited for an order. But he didn't have to wait long in those eager days. Artist and buyer might haggle over a price, for the artist in those days was not shy about making a business deal. And there was work enough for all.

Giotto's reputation grew fast.

He was called to Rome by the Pope in 1298 to do a painting for a mosaic in the old church of St. Peter. But far more important to him than the actual assignment was the revelation of Rome itself. The arches and broken columns and the remnants of Greek and Roman statues come down from antiquity made a powerful impression on the young Florentine painter. He was a plain man who liked solidness and directness. These figures of ancient art were in tune with his personality and they left their mark on his painting. It was this that set him apart, not only from his master Cimabue, but from all the artists of his day.

Giotto was a bluff, hearty man who liked a joke. He had a wife and several children, all of whom, he used to say, were as homely as their father. But about his art he was always serious, and deeply humble. He was by now an acknowledged master, but he never wanted to be called "master." The more he painted, the more he realized he had to learn.

His big chance came when a wealthy merchant of Padua asked him to decorate a chapel—the Arena Chapel, so called because it stood near the ruins of a Roman theater.

It was not unusual in those days for merchants to build chapels, for the glory of God and of their city, and to make the way easier to heaven. To decorate the walls and ceiling of the chapel they would call in the best artist they could find.

So it was that Giotto found himself with an assignment to paint the life of Christ and the Blessed Virgin, and a whole chapel of empty walls on which to do it. If ever he could prove himself to his own satisfaction, this was the time!

Giotto's frescoes on the walls of the Arena Chapel are among the finest paintings in the world. The colors are still fresh and beautiful—lavenders, blues, rose, gray-green. When one steps into the chapel the world seems young. The figures are noble, and every scene is a devout or a tragic experience.

Before Giotto, artists painted their figures not as real people but as symbols. Cimabue's Virgin is magnificent against her curtain of gold, but without an emotion. But Giotto's Mary in *Lamentation Over Christ* is a woman torn with sorrow as she bends over the prostrate body of her dead son. The women around her are

GIOTTO. Lamentation Over Christ. Arena Chapel, Padua.

deeply saddened, the men are filled with pity, and the crowd behind is curious in a very human way.

Unlike the medieval figures and Cimabue's, Giotto's figures have weight and bulk. The earlier ones were flat and two-dimensional. Giotto's are "monumental."

The Arena Chapel frescoes ushered in a new epoch in painting.

Giotto was a fresh strong wind blowing through artistic Italy. He painted in Assisi, Rome, Florence, Padua. He was called to Naples to paint for King Robert of Anjou. And later to Milan.

In Naples he and King Robert became good friends. The king liked to watch him at his work.

23

"Giotto," the king said one day, "if I were you, this hot day, I should suspend my painting for a while."

"I certainly would suspend it," answered Giotto, "if I were King Robert!"

Another time the king asked him to do a picture of his kingdom. So Giotto drew an ass wearing a saddle, and sniffing at a second saddle, which lay at its feet. Both saddles were adorned with the royal crown and scepter. "This," explained the painter, "is an image of your kingdom and your subjects who are always looking for a change of masters."

Such little stories may again be only legends. But they are in character. He was a man without fear or pretense, full of fun and vitality. Boccaccio sings his praises, and Dante, who was Giotto's friend, places him high in the ranks of the *Paradisio*.

In his old age Giotto became chief builder for the Florentine Government, which was not an unusual assignment in those days when a painter could also be an architect, a sculptor, a poet. He designed the Campanile, the lovely pink bell tower that stands beside the Cathedral of Santa Maria del Fiore ("Duomo"). But he died in 1337, before the Campanile was finished.

Giotto forged the first link that binds the art of classical Greece and Rome, a thousand years behind, with that of the Italian Renaissance still a century ahead. He marks the end of the Middle Ages.

After Giotto it was a full hundred years before another painter of equal power entered the story of painting. But during the long interim many artists came and went, leaving behind them many charming paintings.

The Sienese painters are a beautiful example.

Siena, neighbor but enemy of Florence, was a typical city of the Middle Ages, with tall many-storied houses and dark narrow streets, a big cobbled square, and a dramatic, tiger-striped cathedral. It is still a medieval city.

Its art was medieval too—fanciful, dreamy, and deeply religious. In one of their many wars with Florence, when the enemy was at the very gates of the city, the entire populace repaired to the cathedral to pray to the Virgin Mary. So fervent was their combined ecstasy that the inadequate little army rushed forth from the church, charged the far stronger invaders, and routed them. From then on the Sienese artist was dedicated to the glory of the Virgin. He painted her in delicate unearthly beauty. Unlike Giotto he did not ask himself how the Mother of God felt when Her Son was taken down from the Cross. No emotion shows in face or gesture. He painted her calm, remote—and exquisite.

DUCCIO DI BUONINSEGNA (c. 1255–1319) and SIMONE MARTINI (c. 1283–1344) were Siena's most famous painters. The backgrounds of their paintings, like those of the Byzantine, were usually gold. The surfaces were flat, and the figures, the trees, the wings of angels, were all made to fit attractively into their frames, regardless

24

DUCCIO. Rucellai Madonna. Uffizi Gallery, Florence.

SIMONE MARTINI and LIPPO MEMMI.
The Annunciation. Uffizi Gallery,
Florence.

of nature and naturalness. In spirit as well as actual painting, Sienese artists looked back longingly, not to Giotto, but to the Middle Ages.

Masaccio

1401–1428

The great painter who did carry on the tradition of Giotto was Masaccio.

His real name was Tommaso di Giovanni Guidi, but the Italians have a way of changing a person's name just enough to describe him. In this case "Mas" was short for Tom, and the "accio" was a matter of personality. His teacher's name was also Tom. He was called Masolino, "dear little Tom." But our Thomas was not endearing to all people. He was notoriously absent-minded, careless about his dress, and careless about money. He often forgot to collect money that was owing him, and was equally negligent about paying what he owed. "Accio" in his case meant "careless" —Masaccio, "careless Tom." As an indication of the appropriateness of his nickname, he was in debt when he died.

Masaccio was born at San Giovanni Valdarno, about thirty miles from Florence. He had two very good friends in Florence, an architect and a sculptor. Filippo Brunelleschi (1377–1446) was the architect. It was he who built the magnificent dome of the Florence Cathedral, which can be seen from every hillside around the city. To her people the dome means Florence. When they are faraway they say not that they are "homesick" but sick for the Dome. There had never been a dome on a Gothic cathedral. But Brunelleschi went to Rome and studied the vast dome of the Pantheon; he measured, made drawings, and eventually not only designed the dome, but created a new kind of architecture, with pilasters, columns, arches, and cornices. We now call it Renaissance architecture, and it has been used as the model for many of the public buildings that we see about us today.

The sculptor was Donatello (c. 1386–1466). He was the first in this new age to study the human body and the human face. Unlike the graceful pretty curves of medieval figures, his figures had muscles and tissues, and their faces mirrored their emotions.

"Why don't you speak?" Donatello would say to a statue when he had made it in the true image of a man.

Brunelleschi and Donatello and the young Masaccio—these three great artists were friends, all working together in Florence, aided and encouraged by Cosimo de' Medici, adored by the people, stirred up by vigorous Florentine thinking, each eager to do his part in breaking with the old ways and creating the new. What strength and reassurance they must have given one another!

Masaccio learned simple grandeur from Giotto. His figures have the same monumental solidity. But underneath the draperies of Masaccio's figures are real bodies. This is what he learned from Donatello. From Brunelleschi he learned about perspective—that

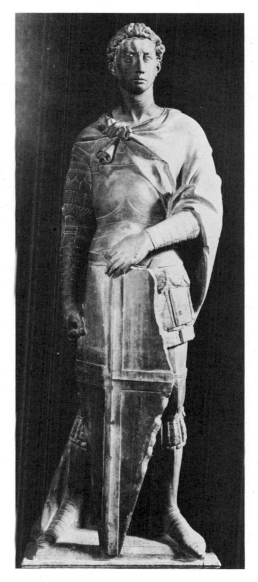

DONATELLO. St. George. Bargello, Florence.

The Pantheon, Rome.

The Duomo from the Podestà Palace Tower, Florence.

Riccardi Palace, Florence.

Strozzi Palace, Florence.

28

is, showing depth and distance in pictures by converging lines. It is a device we accept now without a thought, but one which the early artists had to work out for themselves.

In Masaccio's *The Holy Trinity* we have a remarkable example of perspective. The Cross hangs in an arch, behind which stretches the curved ceiling of a chapel, narrowing in the distance. This is the first painting that has real "depth," with figures in front and figures behind. To the Florentines it was as if they were looking into a room beyond.

Masaccio's most important work was painted for the walls of the Brancacci Chapel of the Church of the Carmine in Florence. Here he painted in fresco the life of St. Peter. Of the several scenes, *Tribute Money* is probably the most famous. There is a look of Giotto in this picture. The solid figures are like his, but there the similarity ends. Here are real people: Christ and His disciples, standing firmly on the bank of a river. They are confronted by a tax collector and are worried and fearful because among them they haven't enough money to pay him. But Christ with a majestic sweep of His arm tells Peter to get gold from the mouth of a fish. This Peter does, to the confusion and surprise of the young tax collector. The colors merge one into another, which is new. There

MASACCIO. The Holy Trinity. Santa Maria
Novella, Florence.

MASACCIO. The Tribute Money. Santa del
Maria Carmine, Florence.

are no bold outlines, and one form blends with another. All this is new. By sheer genius this young painter worked out a way of suggesting air around his figures, which was not done again until the famous Leonardo da Vinci painted nearly two generations later.

Masaccio's most dramatic painting is *The Explusion of Adam and Eve*. Adam and Eve are expelled from the Garden of Eden because they yielded to temptation. They are afraid. Eve weeps, and Adam hides his face. This is the tragedy of a man and a woman facing an unknown world. It is human emotion on a noble scale, which is the true mood of the early Renaissance. Man was depicted in heroic proportion; more tragic, firmer, and more energetic than in everyday reality.

This great artist died at the age of twenty-seven. He was working in Rome when he died, some say from poison, others that it happened in a street brawl. No one knows. What we *do* know is that in the recorded history of art no painter achieved so much in so short a time. For a hundred years to come the Brancacci Chapel with its Masaccio frescoes was the gathering spot for all the intelligent artists of Florence and Northern Italy.

MASACCIO. The Expulsion of Adam and
Eve. Santa Maria del Carmine, Florence.

Fra Angelico
1387–1455

Fra Filippo Lippi
1406–1469

Benozzo Gozzoli
1420–1497

Paolo Uccello
1397–1475

The story of art is like a golden beach upon which the waves never cease to break. One powerful wave rushes far up the sand carrying all before it, followed by many wavelets. Then comes a second strong wave surging up with all the force of the ocean behind it. And again, the smaller ones come in its wake.

After Masaccio there were many waves receding and advancing, sparkling and breaking into fragments of light. Florence was quivering with excitement. Families of wealth wanted pictures, churches were built, artists were besieged with orders.

FRA ANGELICO was one of the most beloved of painters. He was a Dominican monk, called in a later day the "saintly" (Angelico) painter. It was said that he never picked up a brush without praying, and never painted a Crucifix without weeping. But this is probably only a legend. Although he was deeply religious, he was a practical man, and by the time he had become a successful painter he was already head of the Dominican Order at Florence, and would have had little time to indulge in emotion.

Fra Angelico's real name was Guido di Pietro, and he was born in the valley of the Mugello not far from Florence. When he was twenty he went with his brother to apply for admission at the Dominican convent at Fiesole, the little town on the hill overlooking Florence. It was typical of his devoutness that he should choose the strictest of all the monastic orders. A year after entering he took the cowl for good: he become a monk and was called Fra Giovanni.

There is no record of his painting frescoes until he was well along in his forties, but as a monk he undoubtedly did some of the delicate painting needed for illuminated manuscripts. Even in the large important paintings of his later years, we feel the mystery and unworldliness of the old manuscripts.

When Cosimo de' Medici built the large San Marco convent for the Dominicans in Florence, he asked Fra Angelico to decorate it. It was a long seven years' undertaking. Each cell had to have its own picture, its little sermon for the inmate's contemplation. There was even a cell for Cosimo himself, who from time to time liked

32

VIRGINIS INTACTE CVM VENERIS ANTE FIGVRAM PRETEREVNDO CAVE NE SILEATVR AVE

FRA ANGELICO. The Annunciation. San Marco, Florence.

to escape into the convent from the bustle of Florence. Even now there is no spot in the city more peaceful and beautiful and inspiring than San Marco, and the spirit is entirely due to Fra Angelico.

Though Fra Angelico lived in Florence in her most intellectual lively day, his pictures at first glance seem to belong to the Middle Ages, with their roundels of exquisite angels, golden backdrop, and deep mystical religiousness.

Fra Angelico was aware of realism and modern ways. He knew Masaccio's paintings well, and that he understood the problem of perspective is quite evident in *The Annunciation,* with its receding arches and effect of distant landscape. But he chose to recall the old days before art had thrown off the cloak of mystery and devoutness.

33

FRA ANGELICO. The Coronation. San Marco, Florence.

FRA FILIPPO LIPPI. Madonna, Child and Two Angels. Uffizi Gallery, Florence.

FRA FILIPPO LIPPI was also a monk, but not a pious one. He was born in a humble street behind the Carmelite convent in Florence, and as his parents both died when he was still a child, the good monks took him in. But the young lad had two strong impulses, both contrary to the life of the convent. One was to get out and be free to wander through the alleyways of the city and mingle with the people; the other, curious enough in such a lad, was a strong urge to paint. Instead of studying his books he drew pictures in them, and whenever he could he wandered over to the Brancacci chapel to watch Masaccio, the painter, at his work. Nothing could be more characteristic of that time in Florence— when a wayward boy escaped his duties, instead of running off to play or go fishing, he hurried to a chapel to watch a great painter!

Whatever may have been the reason, art, not religion, won out. At seventeen, by an indulgence of the Pope, Filippo Lippi was allowed to leave the monastery forever and return to the streets and doorways of the world of happy folk that he loved so well.

Much as he admired Masaccio, Fra Filippo did not paint in the grand style. He liked grace and charm—not nobility, but prettiness; not gods and goddesses, but people whom he saw in the streets of Florence.

In his *Madonna, Child and Two Angels,* his Christ Child is a husky Italian baby, his Madonna a beautiful Florentine girl, and the angel looking out at us might be any smart city urchin.

He was a rollicking fellow always getting into mischief, roistering, making love, neglecting his work. Cosimo de' Medici was particularly fond of him in spite of his escapades—perhaps because of

FRA FILIPPO LIPPI. Madonna, Child and
Two Angels (detail). Uffizi Gallery,
Florence.

35

FRA FILIPPO LIPPI. Coronation of the Virgin (detail). Uffizi Gallery, Florence.

them. But when he gave Fra Filippo an order for a painting he took the precaution of locking him up in a room of the palace to be sure the picture would be finished. He did it once too often, however. Unable to remain in order, Filippo made a rope of sheets and on it descended out the window to the street. Cosimo never went so far again. A good painter to him was a man of first importance. No matter how long it might take to get a picture finished he would never again risk the danger of losing the artist.

When Fra Filippo was painting the *Coronation of the Virgin* for a convent of nuns, he saw among the nuns a beautiful novice (young girl planning to be a nun). He asked if he might use her as a model for his Virgin. He received permission to do so, fell madly in love, and eloped with her.

Fra Filippo's pretty paintings became very popular. They created a trend that we can trace in galleries among other lesser artists of that same time. He died while painting in the town of Spoleto. The city of Florence insisted on having his body brought back for burial, but the people of Spoleto, having never nurtured a great artist, refused. They kept the body, and built over it a magnificent tomb.

Not all the painters of this effervescing city shared the light-hearted mood and the everyday earthly joys of Fra Filippo Lippi. For PAOLO UCCELLO painting was a serious business.

Paolo de Dono was called Uccello because of his love of birds (*uccelli*). Nothing would have pleased him more than to fill his little house with birds and animals. But all his life through he never could afford the money for their food. So he painted them instead!

One of the reasons for his poverty was his scholarliness. Uccello was the first painter actually to work out the laws of perspective. Giotto, a hundred years before, knew nothing of perspective. Masaccio, as we have seen, used perspective in *The Holy Trinity,* not because he understood the laws that govern perspective, but because, as an inspired artist, he "felt" them.

What Masaccio accomplished with a good eye and possibly with the help of his architect friend Brunelleschi, Paolo now worked out mathematically. Someone had to do the hard work. And to the day he died, at 80, Paolo dedicated himself to that task. He drew ground plans and worked out the rules of converging lines. The more difficult the problem the happier he was. Sometimes he worked all night at his drawing board. Once when his wife tried to get him to go to bed, he called out, "What a sweet thing perspective is!"

Uccello's most famous painting is the *Battle of San Romano,* a handsome picture, but as unreal as a child's world, with its rocking-horse steeds and its forest of spears. The important thing to Uccello was that the spears were so arranged as to diminish toward the vanishing point (perspective) and that the corpse, lying prostrate, front left, was foreshortened (also perspective), probably the first example of foreshortening in painting. We take so much for

UCCELLO. The Battle of San Romano
(one panel). National Gallery, London.

granted now—with centuries of painting experience behind us—
that it is hard to appreciate how difficult the first steps were.

Processions were the delight of Florence, banners afloat in the
breeze, trumpets blowing, horses richly caparisoned, handsome
riders in gorgeous raiment. In 1439, when BENOZZO GOZZOLI
was a young man, Florence staged just such a pageant. The
Byzantine Emperor and Patriarch (the High Priest of Constantinople) were guests of the city and took part in a spectacular
procession, which still winds its picturesque way down through
the mountain roads to Florence and the river Arno—on the walls
of the chapel in the Medici Palace. We see it there through the
bright eyes and the clever brush of Benozzo. This large fresco,
Visit of the Magi, was commissioned by Piero de' Medici, son of
Cosimo. It is fifteenth-century Florence, its gardens, courtyards,
castles, costumes, even its historical personages. The Emperor and
the Patriarch are represented as the two older Magi, and young
Lorenzo de' Medici, grandson of Cosimo, on a white horse, is the
third wise man from the East.

In Pisa Benozzo painted Old Testament stories on the walls of
Campo Santa.

He was a holiday painter, a cheerful good-natured man. He
was a pupil of Fra Angelico, and like his master dotted his
landscapes with birds and dogs and flowers. Though the world
around him underwent profound changes during his lifetime, he
seems never to have lost his serenity. He lived to be 78, and died in
the little house he had bought in Pisa for his old age.

His happy and vivacious pictures were greatly admired in his
own time and are a delight to us today. They are frequently reproduced on Christmas cards.

37

GOZZOLI. Visit of the Magi. Medici Palace
Chapel, Florence.

These paintings of the men who followed Masaccio are not
milestones in the history of art. But they are beautiful pictures,
and they testify to the excitement that was in the air, the urge to
study as well as to paint—in the glorious days of the Early Renaissance.

Piero della Francesca

c. 1420–1492

Piero della Francesca stands forth like an ageless oak tree on the
plain. By painters of today he is considered the greatest of the
Early Renaissance artists, and one of his pictures, *The Resurrection,* has been called by Aldous Huxley the greatest painting in
the world. Yet Piero was forgotten for centuries.

He was born in Borgo San Sepolcro on the upper Tiber. This
is in Umbria, in the heart of Italy, a quiet town surrounded by flat
fertile fields. It was dear to Piero. In spite of his wide travel
throughout Italy—and he was called to many cities, because in
his day he was a very famous painter—he always went back to
Borgo. He became the city councilor. He painted his first im-

38

portant picture, *The Resurrection,* for its town hall, and during the last fifteen years of his life he rarely left it. He was the great old man of Borgo. Its even tenor pervades his paintings.

From this distance Piero della Francesca seems a strange figure. We might easily hurry past his paintings in a gallery. But should we stop to study them, with eyes knowledgeably opened, their extraordinary power would penetrate our consciousness.

The Resurrection has the look of Giotto and Masaccio. It is simple, monumental. But there is an additional something that is pure Piero—a kind of noble serenity. The large quiet figures, with their calm broad faces, seem to belong to eternity. They are motionless, as if miraculously discovered in those very attitudes. The air is one of aloofness, impersonal, unemotional. We shall be reminded of Piero when later we see the paintings of Vermeer in Holland, Velásquez in Spain, and Seurat, centuries later, in France.

It is said that in this picture, the soldier asleep, leaning against the tomb from which Christ has so quietly arisen, is Piero himself. There is an "apartness," a "separateness" about that soldier which might well have fit Piero.

The colors were new to that day—those many tones of soft green in the landscape, the pink of Christ's robe, the ivory of the flesh. The trees are like ancient columns.

Even though forgotten in the period that followed, Piero was appreciated by the art connoisseurs of his day. Many of the ruling families gave him commissions. In Rimini he painted for Sigismondo Malatesta, one of the most ruthless, cruel, unscrupulous of all Italian despots, a *condottiere* (soldier) turned tyrant. He was excommunicated by the Pope and burned in effigy. After his death his son continued on the same path, and murdered his father's wife. Yet in terms of art the Malatestas were a cultivated family.

PIERO DELLA FRANCESCA. Portrait of Sigismondo Malatesta (detail). Rimini Chapel.

PIERO DELLA FRANCESCA. The Resurrection. Picture Gallery, Borgo San Sepolcro.

39

PIERO DELLA FRANCESCA. Portrait of Federigo da Montefeltro. Uffizi Gallery, Florence.

In Urbino Piero painted for Federigo da Montefeltro, who as a ruler was Sigismondo's opposite. Montefeltro was one of the truly great men of the day, statesman, soldier, philosopher, beloved friend of his people. He was not a handsome man. One eye was gone, his nose was broken, he had warts and coarse hair. But in his portrait by Piero one recognizes a true prince of the Renaissance —a man of deep intelligence and unforgettable personality.

Piero himself was a man of many attainments, not only an artist but a mathematician. He painted for a living, and studied and wrote a book on mathematics for his own intellectual satisfaction. In fact, his study of the geometry of objects in space is so exact that it is still found useful by experts in airplane design.

His paintings reached their height in Arezzo. There, in the church of San Francisco, he painted a series of frescoes: *The Story of the True Cross,* of which *Visit of the Queen of Sheba to Solomon* is one of the most charming and graceful. Here, as in *The Resurrection,* are the same eternal impassive values. It is an Olympian world.

The end was none too happy. Piero never married and he must have been lonely. He lived to be 72. He was blind in the last few years so that he could no longer paint, and one of his pupils took the credit for his book on mathematics.

Andrea Mantegna

1431–1506

Mantegna was a great artist, one of the most famous painters of his day. The world was at his feet. Yet he died in tragic poverty.

He was born in Vicenza of poor parents, and, like Giotto, was a shepherd. But while still very young he had the good luck to go to Padua. That was the time when Donatello and Paolo Uccello were both working there, and art was in the air.

There was a certain smart tailor in Padua called Squarcione, who had made quite a name for himself. After he became prosperous, he traveled, collected antique statues, and set up a studio. Here he took orders for pictures and brought together many young boys of talent to paint them. With a shrewd eye for genius Squarcione got hold of young Andrea Mantegna, employed him in his studio, even adopted him as a son. That Andrea turned out to be the cleverest of all the lads goes without saying, and there is little doubt that during his day the studio orders were better executed than at any other time.

All might have gone Squarcione's way had the Bellini family of Venice not come to Padua—the painter Jacopo Bellini, his two sons, Gentile and Giovanni, painters also, and his daughter Nicolosia. Mantegna at once became friendly with the Venetians. He studied with the father, married the daughter, and became the artistic companion of the sons. Whether because of jealousy or rivalry or the loss of a good workman, we do not know, but Mantegna's

MANTEGNA. St. James on the Way to His Execution. Church of the Eremitani, Padua.

relationship with Squarcione came to an abrupt end, and he and the Bellinis left Padua.

The Squarcione collection of ancient statues, however, had a lasting effect on Mantegna's art. As he grew successful he, too, began to fill a studio with antiques, and as a painter he was the most "Roman" of them all. His figures have the solidity of statues. And Roman armor, helmets, and spears are strewn through his pictures. (See the exact legionaries' armor in *St. James on the Way to His Execution*.)

The greater part of Mantegna's life was spent in Mantua in the court of the Gonzagas, who were a family of the greatest distinction. Together the Gonzagas and the Montefeltros (for whom Piero della Francesca painted) give a striking picture of the highest social circle in Renaissance days. These families were taught in the same school, by one of the great schoolmasters of all time. The school was La Giacosa, in Mantua, and like Eton and Harrow in England, was a training ground for leaders of men. The teacher was Vittorino da Feltri, who, though he insisted upon democratic principles and took many pupils *not* of the nobility, was nevertheless keenly aware of his responsibilities toward little Gonzagas, Montefeltros, d'Estes, and the others who, as the Renaissance equivalent of royalty, would one day have to set an example to their people. There was no pampering of spoiled little rich boys, no opportunity for self-indulgence. They had to eat plain food, sleep long, endure cold. They must be physically fit. They rode, jousted, played games hard, and climbed mountains—a new sport for those days. They were taught history, the classics, and mathematics.

At La Giacosa there was no punishment except Vittorino's disapproval, which was punishment enough. Before these young aristocrats he spread the pattern of a truly civilized life, and through them, through their children, and through intermarriages, several Italian courts of that period upheld the highest ideals in leadership.

Nowhere was this prevalence of learning and of good taste more evident than in the court of the Gonzagas. Duke Ludovico made Mantegna the court painter: Mantegna's little toe, he said, was dearer to him than the whole body of most of his subjects, and for the priceless service of his art Mantegna was given a house, fuel, grain, and a salary. In the years of his prime this brought him happiness and contentment. He raised a big family, traveled where he would, gathered together a fine collection of antiques, and painted magnificent pictures. He did for Northern Italy what Masaccio did for Florence.

To flatter a woman in those days you only needed to tell her that she looked like a Mantegna. The special dreamy beauty of *The Madonna of Victory* is pure Mantegna, and the heavy garland of flowers and fruit in the same altarpiece, as in many of his other religious pictures, is also one of his distinctive characteristics.

As he grew old Mantegna became less important to the court. A younger generation came into power and lost interest. The old man's salary was more and more often overdue, and asking for it became more and more painful. But he continued to live there for want of another place, and worked faithfully to the end.

MANTEGNA. The Gonzaga Family (detail). Ducal Palace, Mantua.

MANTEGNA. The Madonna of Victory. The Louvre, Paris.

BOTTICELLI. Self-portrait (detail from The Adoration of the Magi) Uffizi Gallery, Florence.

One by one he had to sell his beloved antiques in order to live. Only one he vowed he would never give up. This was a bust of the Empress Faustina. Unfortunately Isabella d'Este, called the most brilliant woman of the Renaissance and now married to a younger Gonzaga, also loved the Faustina. Day after day Isabella pressed the old man to let her have it, but only when times got too hard and his debts too unbearably heavy, did he at last give in. Soon after that he died. The loss of Faustina was the last straw. He had no further desire to live.

Mantegna was seventy-five, and Isabella was a healthy thirty-two. Hers was an act of self-indulgence and of cruelty, the very traits that the Gonzagas—under the influence of the schoolmaster Vittorino—had tried to eradicate from their court.

Sandro Botticelli

c. 1445–1510

Botticelli stands for romance—the eternally sad and sweet faces of beautiful women, graceful swaying dancers, a world far removed from the humdrum present. To many, Botticelli means Florence and the soul of the Quattrocento.

BOTTICELLI. The Adoration of the Magi. Uffizi Gallery, Florence.

BOTTICELLI. Primavera (detail). Uffizi
Gallery, Florence

POLLAIUOLO. Fighting Men, engraving. Uffizi Gallery, Florence.

BOTTICELLI. The Madonna of the Eucharist. Isabella Stewart Gardner Museum, Boston.

Actually Botticelli was a solid man, tall and rather heavy, with a big face and heavy features; as far as we know, unloved by any woman. He was born Alessandro dei Filipepi, and his father was a tanner, an understanding man who saw at an early age that his son was a genius. He placed him with a goldsmith named Botticelli, hence the name by which we know him. The goldsmith's art was close to the painter's and his master in turn sent the boy over to the studio of Fra Filippo Lippi. Later still, when he was twenty-two, he was apprenticed to ANTONIO POLLAIUOLO, whose paintings were noted for the vigor and muscularity of their figures.

It is interesting to see the influence of both these teachers on Botticelli's early work. Comparing Botticelli's *Madonna of the Eucharist* with Fra Filippo's *Madonna, Child and Two Angels* (page 34) we see that they are the same picture. But instead of Filippo's young woman of Florence with the street urchin grinning out at us, we see a madonna of haunting sweetness (forerunner of Botticelli's later lovely ladies) and a thoughtful meditative boy.

The Allegory of Spring or *Primavera* is Botticelli's most famous and most individual painting. Yet its pattern is obviously inspired by Pollaiuolo's frieze *Fighting Men*. But where Pollaiuolo's lines are all action, Botticelli's are rhythm. *Primavera* is a slow beautiful dance.

Of all the Medici, Lorenzo the Magnificent was perhaps the greatest. Under his golden rule the Quattrocento reached its peak. He established the Platonic Academy of which his grandfather Cosimo had dreamed, and around him gathered all the brilliance of that shining day—scholars and poets and artists, eager young men and elderly sages, grouped around Lorenzo in the quiet garden of San Marco. They came together to discuss the ancient philosophies, to read from the ancient poets, and to write poetry of their own. Lorenzo himself wrote poetry, in the Italian common language, which ranks with the best of his day.

44

BOTTICELLI. Primavera. (See detail, page 43.) Uffizi Gallery, Florence.

Lorenzo was far from handsome. His nose was flat, his complexion sallow. He had a high-pitched voice and practically no sense of smell. But he had everything else—the graces of a gentleman, the wisdom of a good husband and father, the erudition of the intellectual, and a poet's feeling for beauty.

Botticelli belonged to the intimate circle that surrounded Lorenzo. The Magnificent was his friend and his patron, and some of Botticelli's finest pictures (like *Primavera* and *The Birth of Venus*) were painted for private rooms in the Medici villa. Those pictures that today are the mecca for all art-minded tourists were in those days seen only by the privileged few.

Primavera is a classical myth. Venus stands in the center below Cupid, with the Graces and Mercury on her right, and on her left, Flora (Spring, in a flower-sprigged dress), a nymph, and the North Wind rushing on to the scene. In spite of the beautiful ladies, the mood is sad—as the mood of Lorenzo and his friends was sad. They knew that however much they read and studied the past they could never return to it, nor completely recapture its beauty. This longing—this regret for the irretrievable past—Botticelli painted in visual poetry. An exquisite melancholy casts delicate shadows over all his work.

The Birth of Venus (see page 46) is also sad. This is not the joyous goddess of the Greeks, but a wistful creature who—like most Renaissance Madonnas—foresees tragedy and darkness ahead.

All Botticelli women—Flora, Venus, the Graces, the Madonnas —were actually one lovely Florentine. She was Simonetta Vespucci, and her story is the essence of Renaissance romance. Golden-

VASARI. Portrait of Lorenzo de' Medici. Uffizi Gallery, Florence.

45

BOTTICELLI. The Birth of Venus (detail of head). Uffizi Gallery, Florence.

BOTTICELLI. St. Augustine. Ognissanti, Florence.

haired, blue-eyed, ivory-skinned, she was crowned Queen of Beauty in one of Florence's most spectacular pageants. She was married into the enormously rich Vespucci family, and was a cousin of Amerigo, who gave our country its name. Poets wrote verses about her. Guiliano, Lorenzo's handsome younger brother, loved her. And when she died, at the age of twenty-two, all Florence gathered around her bier and wept.

But Botticelli did not confine himself to the sad faces of beautiful women. His *St. Augustine* is thoroughly masculine, a thinking man working on a profound problem—one of the best portraits of an intellectual ever painted.

In 1490, when Botticelli was in his middle years, Savonarola began preaching in Florence against the wickedness of the world. His influence on the painter made for a complete upheaval of the habits, friends, and work of a lifetime. On Florence Savonarola had the impact of a tornado.

Girolamo Savonarola (1452–1498) was a Dominican monk who lived amidst the beauty of Cosimo de' Medici's San Marco, in one of the cells painted by the gentle Fra Angelico. But gentleness was not a characteristic of the fiery Savonarola. He was an evangelist preaching in the public squares, foretelling doom. He denounced the Medicis as rulers, the intellectuals as irreligious, the frivolous, worldly-minded people as sinners. He called upon the Florentines to burn their "vanities"—their jewels, their fancy dresses, their foolish books. And a great bonfire was built in the public square, the Piazza della Signoria, into which the fervent converts hurled their treasures.

Savonarola lived and preached in Florence for eight years. Lorenzo tried to be his friend, but Savonarola turned his back. "This stranger comes to dwell in my house," said Lorenzo, "yet will not stop to pay me a visit."

But Lorenzo had only a short time to go. His arthritis was unbearably painful, and he died in 1492.

After the death of the last powerful Medici (others were to come, but not like these) Savonarola became the sole lawgiver of Florence. He became dictator—a dictator with the spiritual good of his people at heart.

But the mob is changeable. The Pope had long been plotting Savonarola's downfall, and soon, with the backing of powerful Rome, the Florentines, who had once hung on Savonarola's every word, turned bitterly against him. He and two of his disciples—one a willing martyr, the other unwilling—were crucified and then burned before a great crowd in the Piazza della Signoria in 1498—the same square where only a year before penitent Florentines had eagerly made a bonfire of their vanities. Their ashes were thrown into the Arno.

After Savonarola's death Botticelli remained openly faithful to his memory. He lived twelve years longer and continued to paint, but the beauty and the charm was gone.

Botticelli never married, but lived his long life through in his father's house surrounded by relatives. At one time twenty Filipepis—twenty families of relatives—lived on one little alley in Florence!

Pope Sixtus IV called Botticelli to Rome to paint one of the frescoes in the Sistine Chapel, which he did. But he quickly returned to Florence. There he sipped the honey and tasted the dregs of a full Quattrocento life.

Domenico Ghirlandaio

1449–1494

Botticelli and Domenico Ghirlandaio were contemporaries and sometime rivals. They both worked for the Vespuccis. Pope Sixtus asked them both to work on the Sistine Chapel. But spiritually the two artists were a long way apart. Where Botticelli felt the tragedy of time slipping and life changing, Ghirlandaio was always on top of the world, happy, bustling, satisfied. He reveled in gaiety and liveliness. He loved elegant living. Mysticism was not for him, nor religious revelation. In the world of painting, Benozzo Gozzoli, not Masaccio, was his ideal.

The focus of Ghirlandaio's art was Florence and the Florentines. When he painted a story from the Bible it was in terms of the city around him. *The Birth of the Virgin,* painted on the walls of the Church of Santa Maria Novella, represents just the sort of beautiful room that the best Florentine families would de-

FRA BARTOLOMMEO. Portrait of Girolamo Savonarola. New York Historical Society, New York.

GHIRLANDAIO. The Birth of the Virgin. Santa Maria Novella, Florence.

GHIRLANDAIO. Portrait of Giovanna degli Albizi. Rohoncz Castle, Lugano.

light in. The charming young lady dressed in the height of fifteenth century fashion is an actual portrait of one of the Tornabuonis—probably the richest merchant family of Florence.

Everybody who was anybody wanted to get into a Ghirlandaio picture. And the artist never turned down an order, even though his sitters were notoriously careless about payment. His studio was a beehive. The apprentices were instructed to accept every order that came in, even to painting hoops for women's baskets. If the apprentices wouldn't paint them, he, Ghirlandaio, would. "I wish they would give me the walls of Florence to paint! I'd cover them with stories!"

Ghirlandaio was only forty-five when he died. But he had been married three times, had nine stalwart children, and had painted the walls of chapels, churches, and the finest palaces. He was ill only five days—of the Plague. When the rich Tornabuonis heard about it they quickly sent him 100 ducats—of the vast sum they had been owing him for years. But it was too late.

One of Ghirlandaio's loveliest portraits is that of Giovanna degli Albizzi, the bride of Lorenzo Tornabuoni. Here is a Florentine girl at her most beautiful moment, painted at what was also Florence's most beautiful moment. The young bride died that same year; her husband was later beheaded under Savonarola's orders.

Ghirlandaio painted Florence as she was in these last days of her fifteenth-century brilliance. If a change were coming he did not sense it. Lorenzo died two years before he did, and the Medicis were expelled from Florence in the year of Ghirlandaio's death. The golden city was already in decline. Its days of greatness were over, and artists turned their faces toward wealthier Rome.

But it is well to remember the links of that chain which makes up the history of painting. There was one young apprentice in Ghirlandaio's studio of whom the master took little notice. He was an awkward lad, thirteen years old, and his name was Michelangelo Buonarroti.

St. Peter's, Rome.

Chapter 2

ROME

The High Renaissance was the glory of the sixteenth century and of Rome. This was the Italian *cinquecento,* the 1500s, and Rome became the center of the art world because it was rich. It was a city of courts—of the Vatican Papal Court and the small courts of the *condottieri,* families now grown strong and powerful, such as the Colonna and the Orsini. Artists came from all over Italy because there was work for all—decorating the magnificent Renaissance palaces now being built, painting altarpieces for the many churches. But to the Romans an artist was still a craftsman. Politics played a larger part in their minds and lives than art and learning.

Spiritually Rome was a long way from Florence of the early Medicis. Yet painting in the High Renaissance was close to perfection. For these sixteenth-century painters nothing was impossible. The trials and errors of an earlier day were past history. They understood the laws of perspective and the structure of the human form. Only beauty counted now. Not spiritual beauty designed to bring people closer to God, as in Medieval times, not the beauty of the natural world, as in the Early Renaissance, but an ideal beauty that was created in the mind and soul of the artist himself.

The three great names of the High Renaissance are Leonardo da Vinci, Michelangelo, and Raphael. All were living and painting at the same time. They had absorbed everything that the painters before them had so painstakingly learned, and now added a vital magnificent new chapter to art, each in his own powerful way. Together they represent the peak of Italian Renaissance art.

Leonardo da Vinci

1452–1519

Leonardo was a lone star shining far above the world of his day, brilliant as that day and that world was. Only now, in our own era of scientific wonders, have thinkers and scientists caught up with him. He designed a machine that would fly. He invented a screw helicopter and a parachute. He dissected corpses in order to understand the workings of the human body, and made anatomical drawings of the hollows in the head and of the blood vessels that conform almost exactly with the pictures now shown by X-ray. He studied rocks, clouds, trees, plants; he observed the ways of birds and insects. He was one of the supreme painters of all time.

Leonardo was born in Vinci, a little village lying between Florence and Pisa. His mother is believed to have been a servant in a good household, and his father was a notary (lawyer). They were not married, and when the boy was still very young his father

LEONARDO DA VINCI. The Virgin of the Rocks. National Gallery, London.

LEONARDO DA VINCI. Madonna and St. Anne (detail of heads). The Louvre, Paris.

LEONARDO DA VINCI. The Virgin of the Rocks (detail). National Gallery, London.

51

VERROCCHIO. Statue of Colleoni. Venice.

took him away to Florence to be educated. Whether or not the grown child ever saw his mother is not known. But many believe that the beautiful woman's face he painted over and over again was her face. Or his dream of her face. The influence of his mother may have gone very deep.

Leonardo was a child genius. His father recognized this and sent him to the studio of ANDREA VERROCCHIO to be trained. Verrocchio (1435–1488) is better known to us today as a sculptor than a painter. His statue of the soldier Bartolomeo Colleoni, high on a pedestal in a square of Venice, has been called the most magnificent equestrian statue in the world.

One wonders if perhaps he would have painted more had his prize pupil not painted so well. Verrocchio gave Leonardo every chance. In his own *St. John Baptising Christ* he allowed the pupil to paint the landscape and the angel holding the vestment, which are the finest parts of the picture (the angel to the left is Leonardo's, the less poetic, on the right, is Verrocchio's). But Verrocchio was too understanding a man to be small-minded. He encouraged the boy, nurtured his unusual gift, and kept him with him for ten years. Botticelli frequently dropped in to the studio to watch the young Leonardo at work.

Leonardo's home life could hardly have been happy. His father married and raised a family of sons with whom Leonardo must always have felt an outsider. He didn't really "belong."

This sense of not belonging reached into his public life as well. He was not a fervent Florentine (like Michelangelo for instance) or a patriot of any city or any court. He worked ten years in the court of Ludovico Sforza, Duke of Milan. Here he did everything, from playing his silver lute for the duke, to designing fortifications against the French, to painting *The Last Supper*. He invented war weapons for Cesare Borgia, the most unscrupulous figure of an unscrupulous day. In Mantua he drew a profile portrait of Isabella d'Este but did not give in to her whims as poor Mantegna was forced to. At a time when artists competed for more and more orders, he chose to paint very little. When

LEONARDO DA VINCI and VERROCCHIO.
St. John Baptising Christ (*left*) and detail (*right*). Uffizi Gallery, Florence.

called to Rome by Pope Leo X he made mechanical animals for the Pope's amusement instead of painting. He worked beside Michelangelo in the Council Chamber of the Palazzo Vecchio in Florence, but never finished the work. He was sufficient unto himself—this outstanding man of an extraordinary age.

The Last Supper was commissioned by Ludovico Sforza for a Dominican monastery. It took Leonardo three years to paint it, and long before he had finished, the efficient prior of the monastery was frantic with impatience. From time to time he would slip into the refectory and find the artist standing on the scaffold deep in thought. The brush would be in his hand but never touching the wall.

Finally the prior complained to the duke.

Ludovico was an intelligent sophisticated man, and when he asked about the delay Leonardo poured out his almost insurmountable artistic problem. Christ has just uttered the words, "One of you shall betray me!" And the twelve disciples—twelve different personalities, each reacting in his own way—cry out, "Lord, is it I?"

He must paint the face of Our Lord! How could a man be so bold?

And the face of Judas who knew that it was he who would betray Him!

Then Leonardo laughed. He'd paint the prior as Judas!

This superb painting unfortunately began to fade almost at once. It was done in tempera. In tempera, the colors, ground into powder, are mixed into a paste, then applied to wood or wall. In this case, wall. Milan is damp. The wall of the refectory was damp, which was fatal. Only a shadow of the original remains. But the beautiful grouping of the figures, in threes, and the human understanding of those thirteen individual men, make it, in the opinion of many, the greatest painting in the world.

This arrangement of figures in a painting is technically known as "composition." Artists of the Renaissance as well as many artists of today arrange their figures and objects in geometric

LEONARDO DA VINCI. Drawing of Isabella d'Este. The Louvre, Paris.

LEONARDO DA VINCI. The Last Supper. Santa Maria delle Grazie, Milan.

LEONARDO DA VINCI. Sketch of Woman's Head. The Louvre, Paris.

designs, in a circle, a triangle, a pyramid, a quadrilateral, or any of these in combination. When well done this makes for an orderliness and harmony that is most pleasing to the eye, usually without the spectator's consciousness of the device. The superb effect of *The Last Supper* is due in large part to Leonardo's skillful composition. The head of Christ is the converging point of all the architectural lines—of the walls, the ceiling, the door, even the table. The figure of Christ with his downstretched arms forms a triangle. The proportions and the balance have been as carefully studied as the plans of an architect, and then executed with such dexterity as to represent natural beauty. The composition alone would be enough to make that picture a masterpiece.

Mona Lisa, equally famous, is a portrait of La Gioconda, the third wife of an unimportant merchant, Francesco Giocondo. With characteristic patience Leonardo worked on this portrait for four years. Mona Lisa had lost a child shortly before he started to paint her, so he had music played and songs softly sung while he was at work, to dispel her melancholy. It is not hard, as you gaze at her, to imagine in the distance the faint sound of a lute.

54

LEONARDO DA VINCI. Mona Lisa.
The Louvre, Paris.

This lovely portrait has had an odd history. Leonardo took it with him when he went to France to live, and gave it, or sold it, to Francis I. It has been the property of France since that time, and one of the greatest treasures of the Louvre Museum. In 1911 it was stolen from the Louvre, completely disappeared for three years, and was eventually found hidden away in Italy. In 1963 *Mona Lisa* made a short visit of good will to the United States where hundreds of thousands of Americans went to see her. In the Metropolitan Museum alone, there were 1,077,531 visitors.

In most of Leonardo's paintings there is a sense of mystery. This is not only due to the haunting inward beauty of his women but also to his new use of light and dark, of atmosphere, of shadow. This use of light and dark in painting is called *chiaroscuro*. It comes from two Italian words: clear–dark. Leonardo did not invent chiaroscuro but he used it superbly. His shadows, made up of many colors, give a soft mysterious effect, and make his figures full and firm and real. With his scientific perspicacity he understood that an object seen close at hand is more exact and precise than the same object seen at a distance; and with his skill as a painter he was able to make the delicate modulations from dark to light that none had used before him, and by so doing, achieve this effect of elusive shadowy distance. In no painting is this more striking than in *The Virgin of the Rocks* (see pages 50 and 51).

Leonardo was a lone soul. He never married, he lived in many cities and in many courts. He drove himself hard, and in his old age he was weary.

Francis I, the French contemporary of Henry VIII, an equally robust and hearty monarch, seemed to understand Leonardo's strange personality, and in 1515 invited him to France. Although the king had marched ruthlessly against Italy, and Leonardo had built fortifications in defiance of him, he now gladly accepted the invitation. As always he was nonpolitical. The king gave him a home near his own castle of Amboise, and there, after three years of French village life, the old artist died. It is said that when Francis heard the news he wept.

Leonardo left twenty beautiful paintings. Only twenty. But he left 5000 pages of notebooks that make one of the outstanding documents of all time. Here were the anatomical drawings, the machine designs, the sketches of animals and flying machines, music notations, astronomical calculations—the outpourings of a phenomenal mind. Leonardo did his notebooks in mirror writing; and perhaps for this reason they were not deciphered until 300 years after his death.

As he neared his end the unconventional Leonardo concerned himself for the first time with the proprieties. That free spirit that no one had been able quite to capture—the man who never "belonged"—now sought the comfort of a good sound burial. In his will he left money for three high Masses and thirty low Masses, and seventy cents each for sixty mourners among the village poor, to mourn for him and follow his corpse to the grave, carrying candles.

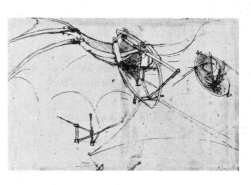

LEONARDO DA VINCI. Designs for Wings of Flying Air Machine. Codex Atlantico, Ambrosiana, Milan.

LEONARDO DA VINCI. Self-portrait. Palazzo Reale, Turin.

Michelangelo

1475–1564

No two personalities could be farther apart than the two giants Michelangelo and Leonardo. Leonardo was tall and handsome, Michelangelo scrawny, short, and homely. All his life Leonardo remained aloof from the fray, Michelangelo plunged into it head-long. Michelangelo went at his art in a frenzy of passion: Leonardo preferred to sketch in his notebook.

Michelangelo Buonarroti was one of a large family that was always hard up. His father, a selfish vainglorious man, objected to his son becoming an artist, yet could not afford to educate him for any other profession, with the ironic result that in his later years of prosperity the son had to support the family. Its members were always around his neck.

Through another boy he managed to get himself apprenticed in the studio of Ghirlandaio. But even at thirteen Michelangelo was critical of the painting turned out at that popular studio. He preferred to go on his own to the Brancacci Chapel to pore over the Masaccio frescoes. (Once outside the chapel he had an argument with another boy which ended in a fist fight. Michelangelo's nose was broken and never mended, adding another blemish to his already unlovely face.)

He wandered about in the Medici Gardens, where Lorenzo the Magnificent had installed some ancient statues for the Florentines to enjoy, and it was here that his luck took a turn. Lorenzo came across him in the garden one day and, after a long talk, was so impressed that he himself took over the boy's education.

MICHELANGELO. Pietà (*left*), St. Peter's, Rome, and Moses (*right*). St. Peter's in Vincoli, Rome.

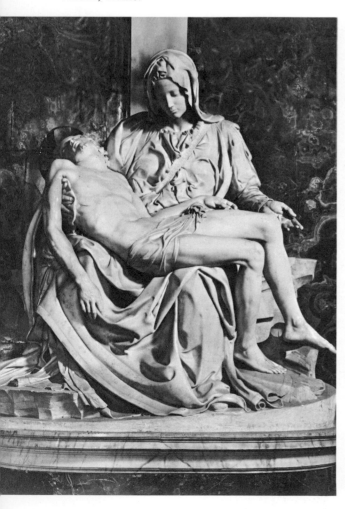

MICHELANGELO. Self-portrait. Uffizi Gallery, Florence.

For four years Michelangelo lived in the Medici Palace surrounded by art and artists, poets and scholars. His overwhelming interest, due probably to the ancient statues, was sculpture, and by the end of the four years, when he was only eighteen, he ranked as one of the foremost living sculptors of Florence. At twenty-one he executed his famous *Pietà,* which now stands in St. Peter's and is one of the sights of Rome. (*Pietà* is the name usually given the picture or sculpture of the dead Christ in His Mother's lap.)

But the foundations were shaking. With Savonarola on his way to power, and the Medicis expelled from Florence, with Lorenzo dead (1492) and the gardens dismantled of their statues, Michelangelo found himself without friends or home. Florence had become a sad place, and the people were pale with fear.

One of these frightened people was Michelangelo. He feared that because of his close association with the Medicis he would be accused of belonging to the wrong side. Politically he leaned toward the side of the poor and the downtrodden, as against those in power. Nevertheless for safety he now fled to Bologna, and from this point on became something of a fugitive, a solitary figure with no close ties.

He already had a sound reputation, and in whatever city he happened to be, orders came in.

It was only under protest, however, that Michelangelo became a painter.

In 1503 Julius II, the newly elected Pope, called him to Rome. Julius was a man of stature. He had united the strong Roman families and so strengthened Rome politically. He made treaties that extended the powers of the Church across Europe. He founded the Vatican library. He gathered around him the great artists of the day. He told Michelangelo that he wanted to build the most magnificent tomb in the world, and with sharp good sense he had picked the only man in the world capable of creating it. These two were vigorous, hot-tempered men, Julius II and Michelangelo. They argued and quarreled. They stimulated each other to a high pitch of effort. If one were happier than the other in this mutual cooperation it was Michelangelo. He looked upon Pope Julius' tomb as the work of a lifetime.

But the tomb was never finished. A towering *Moses* (see page 56) and two captive slaves were done. But by then the Pope had got another idea. Now he wanted the greatest cathedral in the world, and instead of using Michelangelo, who was architect as well as sculptor, he called the architect Bramante from his home town of Urbino to build a new St. Peter's.

Michelangelo was in a rage. Not only was the tomb discarded but a rival chosen. In a state of fury he rushed away from Rome and sent a message back from Florence that if the Pope wanted him he could come and get him.

Julius knew a great artist when he saw one, and he demanded that Florence return the artist to him at once, which Florence meekly did.

The Pope now ordered Michelangelo to paint the ceiling of the Sistine Chapel in the Vatican. Again Michelangelo was furious. He was a sculptor, not a painter! But no one could defy Pope Julius. So the Sistine Chapel ceiling was painted, and one of the mightiest conceptions in art was fulfilled.

For four years Michelangelo worked on the ceiling. He worked alone. He locked himself in the chapel and allowed no one to enter. Only Pope Julius stormed in from time to time, and when the work was half done, he found it so magnificent that he wanted it opened up to the public. Michelangelo refused, whereupon Julius said he would have him thrown off the scaffold.

MICHELANGELO. The Prophet Daniel (*left*). The Delphic Sibyl (*center*). The Prophet Isaiah (*right*). Sistine Chapel, Rome.

MICHELANGELO. The Creation of Man, from the Sistine Ceiling. Vatican, Rome.

To realize the magnitude of this achievement one must remember the vast space that had to be covered, and the extreme difficulties of fresco painting.

In fresco painting the artist had to plaster just as much of the wall or ceiling as he expected to cover in a day. If the plaster was too wet it would not hold the paint, if too dry the paint could not enter the wall and would crumble off. He could not change a line or color, and had to carry in his mind's eye the difference between the color of the drying paint of yesterday and the fresh paint of today. The entire scheme had to be in his head from the first to the last day of work.

Moreover, a ceiling was far more difficult than a wall. Giorgio Vasari, who was Michelangelo's friend as well as his biographer, says that having to look constantly upward as he painted, Michelangelo seriously injured his eyes and for months afterward could read a letter only when he held it over his head. (Vasari, who wrote the famous *Lives of the Artists,* is frequently in error about the artists who lived long before his time, but it is unlikely that he would be so about his friend and contemporary.)

The magnificent Sistine ceiling represents the *History of the World* from the *Creation to the Deluge,* conceived by a great artist and executed by him, alone and unassisted. The gigantic figures have the beauty of Greek gods, but they are gods with the knowledge of suffering that comes from life on earth. They have the austere grandeur of the Old Testament.

The Creation of Man in the very center of the ceiling is one of the most sublime moments in art. The Almighty God of the Universe has flown down from the heavens in his billowing robe,

59

THE LAOCOÖN. Museum of the Vatican, Rome.

RAPHAEL. Self-portrait. Uffizi Gallery, Florence.

his angels about him. Adam, the first man, gently awakened from sleep by the touch of God's finger, does not spring into being. He remains quiet, and thoughtful. Life, which he is about to enter, holds more sadness than joy. But he accepts the inevitable. He is trusting, and, to a degree, resigned.

This is one of the greatest of all works of art. It breathes an ideal radiance. It is infinite and eternal. It has the power to make men dream.

The tenseness in Michelangelo's spirit, mounting sometimes to frenzy, came forth in all his painting. He was present in Rome when the famous statue *The Laocoön* was unearthed, and the twisted fury of that writhing accorded with his own temperament. His own figures turn and sway and gesture. The drama and excitement of this new emotional approach swept through the entire generation of painters who followed Michelangelo. Unfortunately in later years, less gifted artists tried to emulate the master's fervor with the result that after Michelangelo Italian art never quite recovered.

He, too, was a lonely man. Like Leonardo, he never married. He lived alone, ate frugal meals, and worked so hard and long that he was sometimes too tired at night to undress. He was tense and proud, disagreeable and suspicious. He never liked Leonardo, a rival. He accused Bramante of intriguing against him with Pope Julius. He distrusted Raphael. But he belongs to the immortals. Sculptor, painter, architect, poet, Michelangelo was one of the greatest figures in an era of phenomenal men.

He died in 1564 at the age of eighty-nine, the year that Shakespeare was born. He died in Rome, but the people of Florence smuggled his body out and carried it home to Florence. Artists, nobles, bishops, merchants, workmen, farmers followed him to his grave.

Raphael

1483–1520

Raphael Sanzio was a charming, handsome young man, a great favorite with the ladies, whom he liked too; popular with clients from Pope to merchant, a hard worker who fulfilled orders to everyone's apparently complete satisfaction.

He was born in the town of Urbino, the town of Pope Julius and of Bramante. He was too late to have known Piero della Francesca, who painted there for the Montefeltros, but came instead under the influence of PIETRO PERUGINO (c. 1446–1523). Perugino's paintings were very popular at that time because they were so completely pleasant. His madonnas were calm and serene, his saints with their heads slightly bent were infinitely graceful, and the landscape behind them was spacious and quiet.

Raphael quickly advanced from apprentice in Perugino's studio to foreman. He was such a good pupil that it is hard to tell an early Raphael from a Perugino. Even in Raphael's later work, of far greater depth and significance, that quality of serenity remains.

When Raphael was just twenty-one he went to Florence. It was when Michelangelo and Leonardo, the foremost artists in the world, were both painting there in the Council Room of the Palazzo Vecchio, and their work stirred the young man's soul. He had already shown great talent. He was highly intelligent and willing to work hard. Moreover he was a welcome change to the customers —much pleasanter than Michelangelo and more easily approached than Leonardo. So that almost overnight he became himself one of the notable figures in the art world of Florence.

Sometimes affability and willingness to meet all on their own grounds means a compromise with artistic integrity. But not so in the case of Raphael, who was steadfastly true to an ideal of beauty which had slowly been maturing through the years. A century of effort came to its climax in Raphael's beautiful Madonnas (see page 63). They have the sweetness of Perugino, and the pyramidal composition which Leonardo had perfected.

Raphael's Madonnas have become so popular and have been copied and printed in so many cheap color reproductions that we are inclined to take them too much for granted. They look so simple, and they are simple, but it is simplicity attained only from deep thought and care and the most highly developed painting skill in that day of truly great painting. Raphael's art, with its

PERUGINO. The Crucifixion with the Virgin, Saint John, Saint Jerome, and Saint Mary Magdalen. Mellon Collection, National Gallery of Art, Washington, D.C.

RAPHAEL. The School of Athens. Vatican,
Rome.

RAPHAEL. Portrait of Pope Leo X. Pitti
Palace, Florence.

RAPHAEL. Portrait of Baldassare Casti-
glione. The Louvre, Paris.

order and its harmony, its intelligence and its ideal of beauty inspired by Greece is the essence of the High Renaissance.

While Michelangelo was busy painting the Sistine ceiling, Pope Julius called Raphael to Rome to decorate four rooms of the Vatican know as the Stanze of Raphael. On these walls, about 200 feet from where Michelangelo was working his heart out, Raphael was painting allegorical frescoes that sum up the intellectual beliefs and ideals of the Renaissance. In *The School of Athens* we have not only a striking example of his highly developed sense of design and balanced composition, but the spacious Roman architecture and broad arches so beloved of the Renaissance Humanists, and a group of famous philosophers, scholars, and artists who were their special idols.

Raphael now had a workshop of his own in Rome with many apprentices and more work than he could handle. He had orders to paint all the persons of importance and his portraits are as magnificent as his madonnas are beautiful.

He was irresistible to both men and women, in wine taverns and in the homes of the mighty, in all circles of life, in Rome and in Florence.

When he died of a sudden violent fever on his thirty-seventh birthday, he was at the summit of his popularity.

RAPHAEL. The Alba Madonna. Mellon Collection, National Gallery of Art, Washington, D.C.

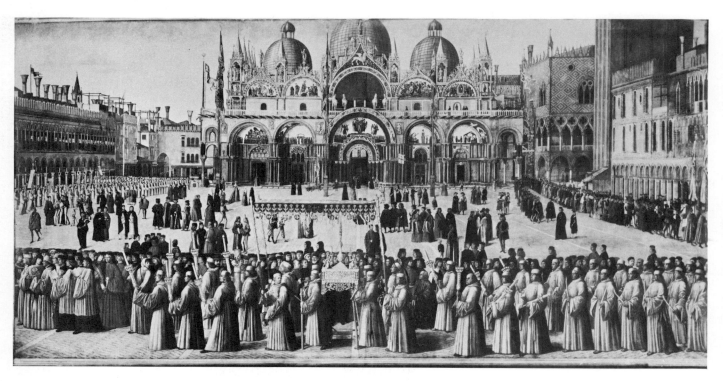

GENTILE BELLINI. Procession of Corpus
Christi. Accademia, Venice.

Chapter 3

VENICE

Venice stood proudly apart from the other cities of Italy, a worldly
city, preoccupied with trade, money-making, and the sumptuous
living that grew out of her wealth. Into her port came ships from
all over the known world. Wool and cloth and wood from England
and Germany and Flanders were exchanged for gum and spices
and silks from Byzantium, Egypt, Syria, Persia, and India. She
was the meeting place of East and West.

Florence had been the art center of the Early Renaissance. During the High Renaissance Rome became the center. But after the
death of the redoubtable Pope Julius II (of Michelangelo and the
Sistine Chapel fame)—in 1513—the focus again shifted. Rome
was in for hard days.

It was in the sixteenth century that Venice came into her own.

She is a lovely city, with twisting canals for streets and small
high curved bridges, old stone palaces leaning over the waterways,
balconies and banners. The handsome square of St. Mark is lined
with arcaded buildings; the church of St. Mark is golden with
mosaics and Byzantine domes; and across from it in pastel elegance rises the Doges' Palace, seat of the mighty.

Her people have always lived a public life. Every feast day in
those early days saw a magnificent procession pass through the
square, resplendent in scarlet and gold. It was—and is—a city of
space and noontime sun.

Even the air of Venice is different from the rest of Italy. Where
Florence is dry and clear, Venice is swathed in mists from the sea.

Through this pearly shroud the southern sun shimmers and glows. The shining water of the lagoon, the constantly changing light of the sky, the vibrating color—all this has had its effect on Venetian painters. Where the Florentines were interested in form, in drawing, in composition, the Venetians subordinated everything to color and light.

A different attitude toward life separated Venice from the other Renaissance cities. The Venetians were not serious. Life was to be enjoyed. Instead of the intellectual alertness of the Florentines, Venice delighted in the senses.

The Bellinis

The famous Bellini family we have already met in Padua; Jacopo, the father, and his sons, Gentile and Giovanni, and his daughter Nicolosia, who became the wife of Mantegna.

Both sons worked in their father's studio and painted very little under their own names until they were in their forties, but as both lived to be very old men they made up for time lost. Gentile (c. 1429–1507), at the age of fifty was called to Constantinople to paint the powerful ruling Sultan, Mahomet II. This was not as strange as it may seem because, as one of the biggest ports in the Mediterranean, Venice was in close touch with the East. .

Giovanni (c. 1430–1516) became the more famous of the two brothers. His early paintings are in the heroic Mantegna style. But

GENTILE BELLINI. Portrait of Sultan Mahomet II. National Gallery, London.

GIOVANNI BELLINI. Madonna with Child and Saints. Church of S. Zaccaria, Venice.

GIORGIONE. Castelfranco Altarpiece. Castelfranco, Veneto.

once back in the moisture and soft air of his native city, he came into his own. The lovely Madonna in the Church of San Zaccaria is a typical early Venetian work, with its mellow light and quietness, its gentle saints, St. Jerome with his book, St. Catherine with the broken wheel—and the beautiful Madonna herself, a light glowing from within.

Giovanni Bellini is usually called the father of Venetian painting though many lesser artists preceded him. For forty years he worked in the Doges' Palace and was the friend of kings, popes, and emperors. He lived to a good old age, and is buried beside his brother Gentile in the great Venetian church of SS. Giovanni e Paola.

During his late years he had a big workshop and many assistants, among whom were two who were destined for even greater fame than their teacher. They were Giorgione and Titian.

Giorgione

c. 1478–1510

Giorgione was a poet among artists, a lute player like da Vinci, young and beloved. The flavor of romance reaches us down through the centuries, even though we know little about the facts of his life. Only five paintings can be positively identified as his work. Yet he is one of the small company of the very great.

He was born Giorgio Barbarelli in a little town just south of the Italian Alps, abounding in meadows and streams and big trees. Though he went to Venice early he painted a magnificent altarpiece for the town of his birth. It is a picture of poetic reverie— the beautiful Madonna with downcast eyes, the contemplative St. Francis, the brooding, unbelligerent St. George, and behind them the lovely idyllic landscape.

GIORGIONE. The Concert (detail). The Louvre, Paris.

GIORGIONE. The Concert. The Louvre, Paris.

Giorgione was a handsome, tall young man always in demand. He was the most popular painter in Venice. The rich sought him out to paint the walls of their houses, but all these paintings, on the outside of buildings as was the style, have faded away. Many women, it is said, were in love with him. One of these, whom he adored, caught the Plague, passed it on to Giorgione, and so caused his death. He died at the age of thirty-two.

At first glance Giorgione's paintings may be confusing. We do not know what title he gave the picture which the world now knows as *The Concert*. He may have been painting a legend no longer remembered. But what we *see* is a valley peopled by the young and beautiful, daydreaming, music-haunted; lacy trees against the sky, floating clouds, a romantic idyllic mood. "Mood" is what we remember about Giorgione—a quality far removed from the intellectual searchings of the Early Renaissance, or the adroitness of Raphael or the might of Michelangelo. It is the mantle of Venice herself.

67

TITIAN. Self-portrait. The Prado, Madrid.

Titian

c. 1477–1576

It is hard to think of the magnificent Titian under the spell of the poetic Giorgione. To the world Giorgione was forever young, and Titian was the old man of Venice. Only five authentic Giorgiones exist, and there are hundreds of Titians. Yet without Giorgione, would there have been a Titian?

Tiziano Vecelli was born in the mountain region of the Dolomites of a well-to-do family who sent him to Venice when very young to get a start in the art world. From the beginning he showed himself ambitious, clever, and an excellent painter. He studied with both Bellini brothers in turn, and seems eventually to have been associated with Giorgione in some kind of partnership. He painted religious pictures and voluptuous pagan ones; and his portraits are a gallery of the important figures of the sixteenth century.

He was a sophisticated man-of-the-world and traveled far and wide. He painted for the d'Estes, the Gonzagas, the Medicis; the Farneses of Rome, King Philip in Madrid, the Emperor Charles V in Augsburg. He kept close to those in power and made a valuable friend of the outstanding publicity man of his day. This was Pietro Aretino, one of the first professional "promoters" in history, a big bully of a man, powerful journalist and notorious blackmailer, but one who recognized genius, and kept Titian constantly in the public eye.

Titian was a good bargainer and usually got the price he asked, but it was not always paid. He did well, however. One reads of

TITIAN. Portrait of Pope Paul III with His Nephews (*left*). National Gallery, Naples.

TITIAN. Portrait of Man with Glove (*right*). The Louvre, Paris.

TITIAN. La Bella (*left*), and Portrait of Pietro Aretino (*right*). Pitti Palace, Florence.

a thousand ducats for this, two thousand for that. (A ducat was worth around two and a half dollars.) He managed to get an income from the treasury of Naples and an annuity from King Philip of Spain—though this, too, was notoriously hard to collect. Painting was big business for Titian. It was also a social wedge. The Emperor Charles V, most powerful ruler in Europe, made him a Knight of the Golden Spur, and his children nobles of the Empire —something that had never happened to a painter before. He kept a lordly household in Venice, as befitted his station, and when he was a widower had his beloved daughter Lavinia as his hostess.

In his early days Titian painted what the Venetians wanted: the opulence of silk and brocade, the gleam of pink flesh, the blue of the sky, the silver of the water. His young noblemen were contemplative and mysterious. His women were of the earth. Where Raphael and Leonardo and Michelangelo had painted an ideal of beauty in their women, Titian painted Venetian ladies of noble families as they were, their hair red-blonde, their dresses heavy with silks and jewels. Blondes were the style in Venice at that time, and though these lordly ladies were seldom seen in public they could sometimes be glimpsed on their balconies drying their dyed hair in the sun.

Titian's frankly pagan pictures, alive with color, made for his immediate popularity. But the painting that created his lasting fame was *The Assumption of the Madonna,* a magnificent altarpiece painted for the Church of the Frari in Venice, which caused a sensation in the art world (see page 70).

Titian's most serious work was done after he visited Rome at the age of sixty-nine. He was deeply impressed with the paintings

69

TITIAN. The Assumption of the Madonna.
Church of the Frari, Venice.

he saw there—the work of Michelangelo and Raphael; and no
doubt recognized that his own belonged to quite another world.
Michelangelo apparently agreed. "Pity that in Venice they don't
learn to draw!" he said. He didn't see that to Titian, as to all the
Venetians, it was not drawing or composition that was of paramount
importance. It was *color*—gorgeous, rich, dramatic color.

After this visit Titian worked with more power and with more
emotion than ever before. He had perhaps become less worldly,
more self-critical, and not so easily satisfied. The *Pietà* was painted
when he was ninety-six, to be hung over his own tomb. It is the
peak of a lifetime of painting and foretells the painting technique
of the future. Color still predominates, but darker color than before,

TITIAN. Pietà. Accademia, Venice.

more somber tones. The edges of the figures are no longer outlined as all figures had been up to this time. They are blurred as one sees in the Impressionists of the nineteenth century. To get the picture's full value one must look at it from a distance—as is true of much in modern art.

The old man was all but indestructible. It took the Plague to kill him, in his ninety-ninth year. His son, who was his assistant, died during the same epidemic, and thieves, under cover of the general confusion, ransacked the Titian home.

Unlike Michelangelo and Leonardo, Titian was not "the universal man" of the Renaissance. He was "just a painter"—but one of the four or five best-known painters in the world, whose work marked the culmination of Venetian art.

TITIAN. The Entombment. The Prado, Madrid.

Tintoretto

1518–1594

Caravaggio

c. 1565–1609

Jacopo Robusti, called Tintoretto, "Little Dyer," because he was the son of a dyer, was a simple man, a good husband, a loyal friend. He lived a pleasant wholesome family life, enjoyed his home, entertained his friends, played music with them. But one would never guess the even tenor of his ways from the tempestuousness of his paintings. They whirl and twist, have torrents of darkness, whirlpools of space, floods of light. When he was an apprentice in the studio of Titian, the master saw some of his sketches and at once dismissed him. Such vehemence was not for him!

"The drawing of Michelangelo and the color of Titian," was the inscription Tintoretto placed over the door of his own studio. These may have been his ideals. But his impetuosity took him far down the stream. In *Christ at the Sea of Galilee* (see page 74) the half-turned figure of Christ gestures in the manner of Michelangelo, and the agitation of the gray-blue sea and clouds we shall see repeated in the work of El Greco.

TINTORETTO. Paradiso. Ducal Palace, Venice.

CARAVAGGIO. The Calling of St. Matthew.
Church of S. Luigi dei Francesi, Rome.

The otherwise mild Tintoretto was always in a frenzy as far
as his work was concerned. In the space of two months he once
finished seven portraits and two historical pictures, each of which
contained twenty figures!

His last picture is the *Paradiso* in the Hall of the Grand Council
in the Doges' Palace. He started it when he was nearly seventy
and finished it three years later. While he was painting, his youngest
daughter, dressed as a boy, stayed on the scaffold with him to
keep him company, chattering and helping when she could. The
Paradiso is like a symphony orchestra made up of many parts—the
largest painting in the world, measuring 2220 square feet! After
this mighty effort the old Tintoretto was ready to stop.

Caravaggio was an Angry Young Man. He was not a Venetian,
though he studied in Venice and was affected by Venetian art,
and he was not among the leading painters of his day. But
the seventeenth century could not have done without him.

He was born Michelangelo Merisi in the village of Caravaggio
near Bergamo in Northern Italy, but his work belongs to no school
of painting. He was sufficient unto himself. When as à student he
was given a Greek statue to study he would have none of it. Instead
he pointed to people passing by in the street. There were his
models! He refused to idealize. *Real life* was his subject.

73

TINTORETTO. Christ at the Sea of Galilee.
Samuel H. Kress Collection, National
Gallery of Art, Washington, D.C.

One of his best known paintings is *The Calling of St. Matthew* (see page 73). Here is an entirely new artistic vision. Light and shadow are of the utmost importance; the hand of Jesus as he points is in strong light, as is the face of St. Matthew; the gamblers are in and out of the shadows. It is dramatic—almost theatrical. The realism of the painting—also distinctly Caravaggio—defeated its immediate purpose. It was painted as an altarpiece but not accepted because St. Matthew was presented as a peasant with dirty feet.

Caravaggio was a violent man, in life and in art, and his paintings, which were frequently harsh in their faithfulness to nature, were shocking to the age in which he lived. But he stuck to his beliefs, and all unknowing became a pioneer. His portrayal of real people and real life, his powerful use of light and shadow had a profound influence on painters of the next three hundred years in Holland and Flanders, in Spain and in France.

He was driven out of Rome on suspicion of murder and fled to Malta and Sicily. He died at forty-nine of fever at Port' Ercole, little realizing the deep impression he was to make on artists of whom he had never even heard.

Tintoretto lived almost to the end of the sixteenth century. Caravaggio leaped over it. As the century waned, so also did the power of Venice. Spain and Portugal were moving to the front in world importance, adding new territories in America and in Asia. The Dutch and Flemish had become a serious threat as traders. Venice was losing prestige. But her wealth still held out. Extravagance and pageantry took the place of robustness. Gondoliers sang as they glided across the canals, chandeliers glittered in gay ballrooms. Venice had become a playground. She was in her decline, but still beautiful.

CANALETTO. Ducal Palace, Venice. Uffizi
Gallery, Florence.

GUARDI. Departure of the Bucentauri.
The Louvre, Paris.

By 1796 Venice had a hundred and thirty-six casinos and a
population that lived for pleasure. It was then that Napoleon, on
his tour of conquest and loot, took her over. He held the graceful
city in low esteem and promised her to the Austrians. All he
wanted was the Greek bronze horses from St. Mark's, stolen from
Constantinople in 1204, by the Venetians themselves, which he
now sent on to Paris; and some gorgeous jewels from the Cà d'Ora
Palace. These he had made into a crown for Josephine.

One should not leave Venice without a last glimpse of her
canals and lagoons as painted by CANALETTO (Antonio Canale,
1697–1768), or the final spray of fireworks sprinkled across the
pale blue sky in the bright accents of Canaletto's pupil, FRANCESCO
GUARDI, 1712–1793—those charming, lighthearted, now priceless
sketches which Guardi as an old man peddled in the Piazzo San
Marco, and could not sell.

75

Chapter 4
THE FLEMISH PAINTERS

North of the Alps art was completely different from the art of the Italians. The northern churches were not broad and open like the Italian, but tall and high, with no wide spaces to fresco. They were medieval Gothic churches. Instead of vast walls, the artists painted on small wood panels, and in this confined space devoted their skill not to gods and god-like men, but to the fine details that they observed in the actual world about them. At the same time the mystery and symbolism of the medieval Church persisted in their souls, as it had not done in Italy. The shadows of a heaven and hell still lurked in their dark cathedrals.

The Flemish were the first of the northerners to awake to art.

Flanders at the beginning of the fifteenth century covered much of the region we know today as Belgium and Luxembourg. Its cities were prosperous and industrious and independent. Bruges, Ghent, Antwerp, and Ypres were big medieval towns with broad market squares and handsome town halls and high belfries. They had early demanded charters and held their own against the encroachments of the nobility, the Church, and foreign invaders. Trade was all important. Bruges, a city of canals, had more ships coming into her docks than did Venice, and Ghent had more members in her wool guilds than Florence. The rich merchants, called "burghers," took the place of the nobles and the powerful *condottieri* of the Italian cities. It was they who financed the many wars of that day, and who also paid for the pictures that were painted.

Not that the Flemish were without glamour. An heiress of the Count of Flanders married a Duke of Burgundy, and together these two powerful families created a court of great splendor. The era of Philip the Good of Burgundy (and Flanders) has been compared to that of Lorenzo the Magnificent in its appreciation of art and culture, but the Italian was considerably more intellectual. Philip created the Order of the Golden Fleece, a famous order of knighthood, and sponsored magnificent tournaments, feasts, and celebrations in which all the people were allowed to take part. The Flemish heartily enjoyed this prosperity and fun, and their village

HUBERT and JAN VAN EYCK. Adoration of the Lamb. Church of St. Bavo, Ghent.

fair (*kermess*) was riotous with drinking and eating and dancing and singing.

Early Flemish art is not intellectual or spiritual. It is of the earth. It concerns itself with people. The rich merchants were practical men who wanted to see themselves in their pictures true to the last hair on the chin. They wanted exact reproductions of the rooms and the fine furniture of their spotless houses.

Throughout the fifteenth century, when Florence and the Early Renaissance were nurturing the experiments of Masaccio and Piero and Mantegna, the artists of Flanders were painting small pictures, symbolic religious subjects, exact reproductions, and—in them all—no ideal beauty, but the faces of plain people, solid and well fed.

Jan van Eyck

c. 1385–1441

There were two brothers van Eyck, both popular painters, born at Maeseyck in Flanders, twenty years apart. Hubert, the elder, taught his young brother what he knew about painting, and his own great masterpiece, *Adoration of the Lamb,* was finished by Jan. It is one of the great Flemish paintings, and though it was finished long after Hubert's death Jan wanted posterity to know that his brother was equally responsible with himself. On the framework are the words in Latin: "Hubert van Eyck whom no one surpassed, began it; Jan, the second brother, with art perfected it."

This remarkable picture is made up of twenty-four panels, which in the course of 500 years have been separated, stolen, sold, have disappeared and reappeared. Finally, as late as the Treaty of Versailles in 1919, they were brought together and restored to the church in Ghent for which they were painted. Since then one panel has again been stolen. Otherwise the altarpiece can be seen today in all its original beauty.

Jan van Eyck was closely connected with the Burgundian court at Bruges for the last seventeen years of his life. Philip the Good, Duke of Burgundy, was his patron and his friend. He was godfather to Jan's child, and after the death of Philip's wife, Jan took on the intimate assignment of journeying to various countries to paint the faces of promising candidates for Philip's second wife. Isabella of Portugal was the eventual choice.

Van Eyck's best-known picture, one of the most famous pictures in the world, is *Jan Arnolfini and His Wife* (see page 78), the charming portrait of two serious young persons on their wedding day. That the painter himself was a witness of the event is stated in the panel above the mirror: *Johannes de Eyck fuit hic, 1434* (Jan van Eyck was here, 1434). The details are infinite—the chandelier, the chair back, the bed hangings, the brocade of the dress, the fur, every hair of the little terrier—all painted on a surface less than two feet wide, and brilliant in color as no paint-

The Belfry, Bruges.

JAN VAN EYCK. Jan Arnolfini and His Wife. National Gallery, London.

ing had been before it. Never before had texture been made so real and so important. Never before had detail been so exact. In fact both these characteristics became the hallmarks of Flemish art.

Jan van Eyck is to Flemish painting what Giotto was to Italian. He gave it its start. He was a great painter for any period, and he made one far-reaching technical contribution. Paint in those days was not in tubes, but in raw pigments which had to be ground up daily. Up to that time the ground-up pigment had been mixed with egg to make a paste. But Jan van Eyck perfected a new method which has lasted down to this day. He mixed the pigments with oil instead of egg.

This use of oil had been attempted before, but van Eyck was the first to use it successfully and for a time it was kept a secret among Flemish artists. Oil made for greater smoothness, greater brilliance, more variety. An artist could blur lines if he wished, and thin down or thicken up the color as he pleased. Where the Italians had produced the effect of distance by the use of perspective lines, the van Eycks, who did not completely understand perspective, got their effect by making the faraway landscape lighter and mistier. Most important, oil paint lasted. To this day, after 400 years, the Flemish paintings are as bright as they ever were, while too many of the magnificent Italian works have gradually faded away.

The van Eycks represent the first great wave that rushed up on the shore of Flanders. Lesser waves followed it, and in the museums we find the works of several painters who came after Jan van Eyck.

HUGO VAN DER GOES (c. 1440–1482), painted in the second half of the fifteenth century. He was a melancholy man, it is said, who suffered all his life from a sense of guilt, and eventually entered a monastery to do penance. His most famous work, painted in Bruges for a rich Italian businessman is the *Portinari Altarpiece,* which now hangs in Florence with the most revered of the Italian masterworks. An air of gentle sadness pervades the figures of Mary and the angels, with the rough realistic shepherds as dramatic Flemish contrast.

VAN DER GOES. Portinari Altarpiece. Uffizi Gallery, Florence.

SOUTHERN FRENCH MASTER. The Avignon Pietà. The Louvre, Paris.

The Avignon Pietà is not a Flemish picture, but it shows the influence of the Flemish school. It was painted by an artist, now unknown, between 1465 and 1470, and found near Avignon in France. It is one of the great paintings of the world, with the devoutness and medieval purity of a van der Weyden and the same deep-lying drama: the curved, white body of the dead Christ, the unbearable grief in the faces of the two women, the tenderness of St. John. Even the figure of the donor at the far left does not distract from the intensity of the scene. He has come from another world, as it were, and in no way touches the terrible tragedy upon which he looks with us.

Not so important in the actual history of painting, but too charming to pass up, are the works of HANS MEMLING (c. 1430–

MEMLING. Mystic Marriage of St. Catherine (center panel). St. John's Hospital, Bruges.

79

VAN DER WEYDEN. The Descent from the Cross. The Prado, Madrid.

1495), who was possibly a pupil of van der Weyden. The story that has come down is that one cold night in January 1477 a soldier, back from the battlefield, knocked on the door of St. John's Hospital in Bruges, and asked for lodging and rest. The monks took him in, and to repay them—in the calm quiet of the monastery—the visitor painted a group of masterpieces.

True or not, Memling permeates St. John's. There hang many of his gentle saints and the exquisite *Mystic Marriage of St. Catherine* (see page 79). This is a triptych, a painting in three panels. The beautiful childish face, the pearly white upraised hand, the elegant gown, are the essence of romance, the stuff of dreams.

Memling was probably a pupil of ROGIER VAN DER WEYDEN (c. 1400–1464). Van der Weyden was not so revolutionary an artist as van Eyck—he did not start very much that was new— but he had a far greater influence on the painters of his day. His pictures gave people the drama and excitement they loved. *The Descent from the Cross* is religious art in the medieval spirit, but it also has the details that create the "look of life" for which the Flemish are famous. The weeping women and the calm, pitying old man tell a sad story. Their appeal is strong and dramatic. Very famous in his day, van der Weyden was invited to several ducal courts in Italy, and visited and painted in Rome, Florence, and Ferrari.

The Bruegels

With Pieter Bruegel (c. 1525–1569) comes a new breath of life. For the first time we can laugh. Here are children playing games, people eating and drinking, peasants enjoying themselves, men sleeping—snoring—in a hayfield, dogs and cats and chickens. Bruegel painted scenes from ordinary life, which are known as *genre* pictures.

But it is only at first that we laugh. Bruegel himself was not lighthearted. He painted hundreds of persons laughing, crying,

BRUEGEL. The Wedding in the Barn.
Gemäldegalerie, Vienna.

working, scolding, suffering, but his purpose was always to show up foolishness or injustice. *The Wedding in the Barn* is a scene of lively merrymaking, quite amusing on the surface. But close examination shows that the complacent bride is rather stupid, the child in front is the picture of gluttony, the emptied mugs, the overworked waiter, and the heavy faces of the guests all suggest greed and vulgarity. Bruegel not only shows us how the wedding looked, but *what he thought of it*. He had the gift of satire.

Pieter Bruegel, called the Elder, was born a peasant but did not stay one long. He studied painting and married his master's daughter. He traveled to France and to Italy, and eventually

BRUEGEL. The Carrying of the Cross.
Gemäldegalerie, Vienna.

JAN BREUGHEL. Flowerpiece. Rijksmuseum, Amsterdam.

RUBENS. Self-portrait. Gemäldegalerie, Vienna.

settled down in Brussels. He knew the world of his day. And he found it cruel.

This was the time when the Emperor Charles V and Philip II of Spain were trying to hold Holland and Flanders (the Netherlands) for the Catholic Church. They appointed as governor the Duke of Alba, a Spaniard, who between 1566 and 1572 hanged and beheaded 18,600 of the inhabitants. Bruges and Ghent became deserted cities, the weavers migrated to England, and horses ate the grass growing up between the cobbles in the Antwerp streets.

It was a dangerous time to portray cruelty and injustice, but that is what the intrepid Bruegel did. In *The Carrying of the Cross* (see page 81) he pictured the Spanish atrocities by means of a Bible story. Gallows are scattered over the landscape, the soldiers moving toward the Cross are in the uniform of the Spanish infantry, the people are clearly in agony. Artist that he was, Bruegel managed to unify this vast plain with its hundreds of figures into one mighty story of human rebellion, dramatic and horrifying.

Pieter's son Jan Bruegel (1568–1625) became famous for his flower paintings. After Pieter, the Bruegel dynasty lasted over a hundred years, all its members good painters, and a strong influence upon the artists to follow. None of the family, however, was so great as the original Pieter the Elder (who lived to be only forty-four years old!). It was the later members of the family who changed the spelling of their name to Breughel.

Jan, the son of Pieter, was sometimes known as "Velvet Breughel," and worked in the studio of Peter Paul Rubens, where the two became good friends. There are several pictures in which the human figures are painted by Rubens, and the birds and flowers by Jan Breughel.

Peter Paul Rubens

1577–1640

The third mountainous wave that swept across Flanders and well-nigh flooded Europe was Peter Paul Rubens, born nearly two hundred years after his fellow countryman, the contained, dignified, exact Jan van Eyck. Rubens was the greatest painter of his day.

But it is not easy in our day to adjust to his pictures. Accustomed to slenderness as an attribute of beauty, we are apt to find his women too fleshy. His pictures seem too big, his canvases overcrowded; too much is going on.

Rubens needs study.

For one thing he flowered in the seventeenth century, and the seventeenth century saw the development of the Baroque style in art—in painting, in architecture, in music. Baroque means movement, intensity, force. Baroque buildings are enormous, Baroque paintings are vast, with figures that swirl onward

JAN BREUGHEL. Flowerpiece (detail).
Rijksmuseum, Amsterdam.

and upward. In music the organ is definitely Baroque, with its vibrancy and multiplicity of overtones. The essence of the Renaissance, both in music and painting, is the clear lute of Leonardo. Baroque painters preferred tumult and passion to order and harmony. Where Raphael arranged the composition of paintings into a pyramid, the Baroque painter loved diagonals. Rubens himself by his very nature was Baroque—a joyous exuberant man, abounding in energy and vitality.

He was born during the dangerous days of religious tension when the Protestant Reformation was at its height. This great revolt against certain medieval Church practices continued through much of the sixteenth century and led eventually to the emergence of the Protestant Church.

As the Netherlands was divided at this time into Protestant Holland and Catholic Flanders, so also was Peter Paul's family divided. His father was a Protestant and his mother a Catholic. Since his father died when he was ten, the child was brought up in the Catholic Church. As man and diplomat he became the confidant of Catholic kings, and as a painter he became the great exponent of Catholic art. With the Reformation spreading through the countries around Flanders, Rubens continued to paint altarpieces.

He was an attractive child, and his mother succeeded in placing him as a page in the court of a princess, where he spent his fourteenth year. Here he learned to speak French fluently. But the court frivolity bored him. Even at fourteen he knew that he wanted to be a painter. And his mother gave in.

For nine years he worked hard in three Antwerp studios, and at the age of twenty-three received the title of Master in the Antwerp painters' guild. Once on his own, he headed for Italy. Actually he mounted a horse and started off—probably at a gallop—for Venice.

It is a long way, over the Alps, from the land of the north to the sunny land of the south.

Italy came up to his highest expectations and he was as popular with the Italians as they were with him. He studied all the great masters, and received many commissions. He worked eight years for the Duke of Mantua, even going on diplomatic missions for

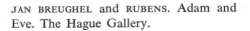

JAN BREUGHEL and RUBENS. Adam and Eve. The Hague Gallery.

RUBENS. Descent from the Cross. Cathedral, Antwerp.

him to Rome and Madrid, always studying, always painting. More than any other Flemish painter Rubens shows the influence of Italy, yet he never lost his Flemish real-life touch. He did not try to imitate the Italians. He wanted only to rival them.

By the time he returned to Antwerp he was famous. Peace had settled over Spain and Flanders. He became court painter for the Spanish Regents Albrecht and Isabella, and he married. It was the beginning of seventeen years of complete happiness.

Isabella Brant was his beautiful young wife, whom he painted over and over again, and they had three beautiful children, whom he also painted many times.

Rubens was an elegant figure, a gentleman, tall, fair, with auburn hair which he kept carefully brushed, a trim beard and ruddy complexion, a man brimming with life, at the same time amiable and kind. He shone in any society and was an intimate of some of the most important men and women of his day.

He was a superb painter all his life, and a successful diplomat for many years. Albrecht and Isabella sent him to Philip of Spain on a delicate mission concerning Spain, the Netherlands, and England. He stayed in Madrid nine months awaiting the king's decision, but was never idle. He painted for the court and became a friend of the young Velásquez, whom he persuaded Philip to send to Italy to see the great art treasures.

When finally Rubens got to England he found in Charles I a man who spoke his own language. "Of all princes," said Rubens, "he is the most enthusiastic amateur of painting in the world." Charles was indeed an outstanding connoisseur and collector of art, as the list of his paintings, which were scattered and destroyed twenty-four years after the collection was completed, will show. He commissioned Rubens to paint the ceiling of Whitehall banqueting hall, knighted him, and on his departure presented him with a diamond ring and a diamond chain to wear around his hat!

But probably Rubens' greatest royal commission was from Marie
de' Medici, wife of Henry IV of France, who chose the Flemish
Rubens, to the consternation of all the French artists, to decorate
her new palace, the Luxembourg. This was an enormous undertaking. He painted twenty-four huge canvases (which now occupy
an entire gallery in the Louvre) depicting Marie de' Medici's none-

RUBENS. The Apotheosis of Henry IV.
The Louvre, Paris.

too-moral life in terms of allegory. They are a pageant of sump-
tuousness where goddesses mingle with humans in a profusion of
color and movement. It took him four years and many journeys—
again on horseback—from Antwerp to Paris, Paris to Antwerp.

Rubens was one of the most popular painters that ever lived and is
said to have made as much as a hundred gold florins (about $100)

87

RUBENS. Madonna and Saints. Church of St. Jacques, Antwerp.

a day, phenomenal for that period. The Russian court once gave him an order for 300 pictures. But none of this dazzled him.

He had a palatial home, a garden with fountains and grottoes and peacocks, a stable of Spanish horses. He liked good living. But he remained a hard worker. He got up at four in the morning all year-round, went to Mass, then painted in his studio as long as good light lasted. Late in the afternoon he rode around his estate. He was a devoted husband and father, spontaneous and joyous as his paintings. Not until Renoir shall we find such another.

Rubens' great sorrow was the death of his wife in 1626. In 1630 he married again, this time the charming sixteen-year-old Helena Fourment, who, like his first wife, became his model. It is interesting to note that something of both these two dearly beloved wives appears in all the women he painted.

Most of Rubens' paintings were done for altars facing the congregation. The color and the sweeping waves of motion were designed to be seen by large groups of people. This he liked. "I must confess that my natural talent lies in the direction of work on a large scale, not in turning out small curiosities. . . ."

His brushwork is world-famous. He did not draw. He painted. With his brush he brought life to paint and canvas. Through the broad sweep of that brush came the man's personality with all its vitality, force, and joyousness.

Rubens belongs to Antwerp. His tomb is in a small chapel in the Church of St. Jacques. Behind the main altar hangs one of his last pictures, *Madonna and Saints*. This is actually a painting of his family. Isabella Brant holds the child. Helena faces her. His daughter, his niece, his father, and his grandfather are all present, and Rubens himself is St. George in armor.

No individual could have painted all that is assigned to Rubens. (He left 1500 paintings!) But he had various ways of getting through his mountains of work. For some pictures he made the design and let his assistants do the actual painting. For others he let them prepare the painting and he himself added the famous life-giving brushstrokes. But in all cases the procedure was specified to the buyer.

Assigning work to assistants was regulation practice and good business. Yet one cannot help remembering that Michelangelo did the entire Sistine Chapel ceiling alone.

Rubens' best assistant was ANTHONY VAN DYCK (1599–1641). To have lived so close to the great Rubens must have been difficult, especially for a painter as talented as Van Dyck. At first he painted like Rubens. Like Rubens he went to Italy to study, painted in aristocratic circles of Genoa and Mantua, and in time followed Rubens to the court of Charles I of England.

There he came into his own. Charles made him court painter, knighted him, and gave him a studio in London and a villa in the country. Van Dyck lived to the hilt—with fine clothing, coach-and-four, thoroughbred horses, music, art, and pretty ladies about.

In return for Charles's generosity Van Dyck made him and his court immortal. He painted the king forty times and made his cavalier courtiers as familiar to us as the German Holbein made the more vigorous court of Henry VIII. Van Dyck was not a robust healthy man, which may account for the rather melancholy elegance of his portraits. But the courtiers liked this aristocratic pallor. Everyone wanted to look as noble as a Van Dyck.

Like Rubens, he maintained a thriving workshop with many assistants. He made appointments, like a doctor or a dentist. He would work an hour on one sitter, then dismiss him and work on another. He would make several sketches in one day, then turn them over to his assistants, who painted in the silks and brocades and lace of the sitters' magnificent garments. (For those aristocratic hands he had models of both sexes in his own house.)

After the death of Van Dyck, the art of Flanders that had flourished 300 years gradually died away.

VAN DYCK. Portrait of the Artist (detail). Metropolitan Museum of Art, New York, Jules S. Bache Collection, 1949.

VAN DYCK. Portrait of Charles I. The Louvre, Paris.

89

Chapter 5

THE GERMAN PAINTERS

Germany's golden age of art was in the sixteenth century. The centers were Augsburg and Nuremberg; its best known artists, Dürer and Holbein. Nearer to Italy than Flanders or Holland, her artists were better able to visit Northern Italy. They knew the works of the Northern Italian masters, and adopted some of the Italian techniques. But the German point of view remained a world apart from the Italian. In art it was not beauty that the Germans sought, but a spiritual lesson. They were moralistic people, tinged with the mysticism and the fantasies of the Middle Ages.

Albrecht Dürer

1471–1528

Albrecht Dürer, Germany's finest artist of the sixteenth century, is one of the few early painters whom we know well. He kept a diary. He was an ardent letter writer. He wrote books. He painted his innermost thoughts into his pictures, frequently painted himself, and signed his works with his now famous monogram.

Dürer was born in Nuremberg, that old medieval city of high roofs and narrow, cobbled streets, which in the sixteenth century was the cultural link between Germany and Northern Italy. He was the third in a family of eighteen children. "My mother kept us all, with great care, from sin," he was wont to say. He learned the goldsmith's trade from his father at an early age. But he preferred to draw.

When the time came for his *Wanderjahre* Albrecht made straight for Italy. (*Wanderjahre* was the "year of journeying" which young German craftsmen used to take—if they could afford it—before they married and settled down.) Italy was a revelation to Dürer. He studied the works of Mantegna and the Venetians, talked with many painters, and observed the high regard in which all artists there were held. When he returned to Nuremberg he was more than ever determined to become an artist.

But the times were troubled. The first rumblings of the Protestant Reformation had already begun in Germany, and religious painting was being frowned upon. Before this time altarpieces had been the painters' bread and butter, as well as the basis of their fame. Now there were no church orders.

Dürer was just twenty-three, and recently married to a girl of his parents' choosing. Apparently the marriage was not a happy one. Agnes, his wife, was said to be a "nagging sour-face," and Dürer seemed to take every opportunity to be away from home. But at this stage he was young, life lay ahead, and he had to make a living. So, with practical good sense he turned to the one form of art still popular. He took up book illustration.

DÜRER. Self-portrait. The Prado, Madrid.

SCHONGAUER. Holy Night, engraving (*left*).

DÜRER. The Knight, Death and the Devil, engraving (*right*). Metropolitan Museum of Art, New York, Dick Fund, 1943.

The invention of movable type (printing) had by now made books available to all who could read, and book illustrations were much in demand. They were of two types: woodcuts and engravings. In woodcuts, the older form, the artist cut out of a block of wood everything that should not appear in the final picture. He then covered the block with printers' ink and pressed it on the paper. The ridges of the block made his picture.

The engraver on the other hand used a copper sheet and cut his picture on it with a sharp steel instrument called a "burin." The parts he wished to have printed were indented. This sheet was also covered with ink and pressed down. The engraving allowed for much more detail than the woodblock, and made for much finer work.

The greatest master of engraving in the fifteenth century, and, as such, one of the most profound influences on Dürer, was MARTIN SCHONGAUER (c. 1453–1491). Under Schongauer's steady hand the "burin" reproduced textures as true to life as those painted by the Flemish in oil. We see these in the wood and plaster, flowers and fur, skin and wrinkles of *The Holy Night*. His compositions for book illustrations were as carefully worked out as for an altarpiece.

In his year of wandering Dürer visited Schongauer's studio in Colmar (unfortunately after Schongauer's death), and there studied this technique of copper engraving and made it his own.

Dürer's engravings were never surpassed, and in their turn exerted a powerful influence on future artists. One of his most famous engravings is *The Knight, Death and the Devil*. The knight symbolizes the life of action beset by evil, the city on the high cliff is his heavenly destination; the devil lurks behind.

DÜRER. Monogram (detail from The Knight, Death and the Devil, engraving). Metropolitan Museum of Art, New York, Dick Fund, 1943.

DÜRER. Adoration of the Magi.
Uffizi Gallery, Florence.

Dürer was a visionary and a thinker. There were no limits to his curiosity. "I want to know something of all things," he once wrote. In that way he was like Leonardo. He visited Italy twice. He studied perspective and anatomy in true Renaissance style, and wrote books about them. But he remained a northerner. The da Vinci feeling for beauty and the Florentine delight with the world were left out of the makeup of this rather melancholy German. He came from a sterner climate, dominated by dark-shadowed forests and the moral severity of the Luther revival.

He was already famous beyond his own country when he visited Venice, and there he was received with open arms. Giovanni Bellini, the master, welcomed him, a rich Venetian banker commissioned him to paint an altarpiece, and the Doge offered him an important post with large salary.

Dürer basked in this praise and appreciation. "How I shall freeze after this sunshine!" he wrote home. But he nonetheless returned to cold Nuremberg.

Although he was best known in his day as a master of black and white, his few paintings rank with the best. *Adoration of the Magi* is a magnificent altarpiece embodying fully the spirit of northern art. The textures are painted with painstaking care—the rocks in the ruin, the wood of the stable, the cloth, the fur. The

92

visiting Magi are serious men, deeply moved by this stupendous event—in contrast to the stately heraldic Magi of the Renaissance Gozzoli pageant (see page 38). The Virgin is not exquisite as an Italian would have painted her, but "aware." The picture is a study of character, which is very German, and of people and objects so real that we know how they feel to the touch, which is characteristic of all the northern painters. Above all, it is a very personal interpretation. It is Dürer's, and only Dürer's.

Small animals had a particular appeal for Dürer. It was a medieval twist in his nature, but the execution was truly Renaissance in its scientific exactness.

Two years before his death Dürer offered his beloved Nuremberg, as a parting gift, a two-panel painting of four saints. These represented the four temperaments of man: Peter, the fiery, John, the melancholy, Mark, the earthy, Paul, the cheerful. They are nearly life-size, their robes are simple, their nobility is monumental.

Dürer died suddenly at the age of fifty-seven. While in great pain he made a drawing of himself pointing with one hand to a spot on his body. "Where the yellow spot is, that is the seat of my illness." He was articulate to the very end.

DÜRER. The Madonna of Many Animals, watercolor. Albertina, Vienna.

DÜRER. Apostles John and Peter (*left*), and Apostles Mark and Paul (*right*). Alte Pinakothek, Munich.

93

Grünewald

c. 1475–c. 1530

We know as little about Grünewald as we know much about Dürer. Even his name was forgotten for three hundred years (he was born Matthias Gothardt Neithardt). But one of the noblest religious pictures in the world has been assigned to him: the Isenheim Altarpiece in Colmar, Alsace. Although it was painted during Dürer's day, while Michelangelo was working on the Sistine ceiling, and Raphael on the Stanzas, the Altarpiece belongs to the Middle Ages. It is a sermon.

The Isenheim Altarpiece consists of a group of panels painted on both sides. When closed, the center panel depicts the Cruci-

GRÜNEWALD. The Crucifixion from the Isenheim Altarpiece. Unterlinden Museum, Colmar.

fixion. It is unutterably sad. Christ has suffered agonies. His hands have stiffened in twisted torture. The world is dark and the women weep. The artist has painted from the depths of his own passion.

Opened up, the panels are a blaze of glory. Here is the shining Annunciation, the Mother and Babe and the celestial orchestra, and Christ soaring into the heavens in a burst of light: the Resurrection.

The church of Isenheim was never closed. The sick and the poor were welcome. Lepers and victims of the Plague went to the altar to pray, hoping for a miraculous cure.

Grünewald himself is believed to have died of the Plague—in Halle, Germany. He was buried outside the walls, with no stone to mark his grave.

Hans Holbein, the Younger

c. 1497–1543

Holbein means Henry VIII to everyone who knows the famous picture of that robust king in all his magnificence. But Holbein did far more than paint a king.

He was born Hans Holbein in Augsburg, the son of a painter (hence "the Younger"), who far outstripped his father. He was a generation younger than Dürer, and where Dürer had felt only the restless beginnings of religious strife, Holbein, as an artist, was its victim. By his day the Protestant followers of Martin Luther

GRÜNEWALD. Celestial Orchestra (detail) from the Isenheim Altarpiece. Unterlinden Museum, Colmar.

HOLBEIN, THE YOUNGER. Self-portrait. Uffizi Gallery, Florence.

95

HOLBEIN, THE YOUNGER. The Virgin with the Family of Burgomaster Meyer. Darmstadt Museum.

in Germany had forbidden all religious paintings and even objected to wall decorations in their homes as frivolous luxuries. It was a sober period with nothing left for the artist but book illustration and portrait painting.

When he was seventeen Holbein moved to Basle, Switzerland, which had not yet been noticeably affected by the Reformation and was for the moment the center of European culture. He worked there off and on for the next twelve years, and painted one sublime altarpiece before the blow fell and all religious art, even

HOLBEIN, THE YOUNGER. Erasmus. The Louvre, Paris.

there, was forbidden. *The Virgin with the Family of Burgomaster Meyer* is as lovely a composition as any Italian altarpiece, with the added exact portraiture so dear to the northerners.

It was 1526 when the Reformation clamped down on Basle. Pictures were removed from churches, several by Holbein were smuggled out to other towns, and it became dangerous for him or any other artist to remain in the city. Sculptors began to carve furniture instead of statues.

Holbein had an internationally powerful friend, the famous Dutch scholar Erasmus, who was at this time living in Basle, and he gave Holbein an introduction to the Chancelor for Henry VIII of England, Sir Thomas More. "He is going to England in the hope of making money," wrote Erasmus with frank simplicity. And the hope was more than justified.

In 1528 Holbein hurried back to Basle, bought a house in which to leave his wife and children, and once more departed for London, where he remained for the rest of his life. In *The Artist's Wife and Children,* which he painted that year, the sadness of his wife's face suggests a foresight of the lonely years to come, for he apparently saw her only once or twice again on short visits.

On his return to London, Henry made him court painter. The figures of the court which we know so well—of Henry and his wives and their children—we know through the authentic brush of Hans Holbein, who can be called one of the world's greatest portrait painters.

HOLBEIN, THE YOUNGER. Portrait of Henry VIII. National Portrait Gallery, London.

HOLBEIN, THE YOUNGER. The Artist's Wife and Children. Museum, Basle.

97

HOLBEIN, THE YOUNGER. Christina of
Denmark. National Gallery, London.

His portraits may not have the color and the sublety of Venetian portraits; the sitters do not smile or laugh or scowl as they were to do later in the portraits of Frans Hals. Unlike his fellow Germans, Dürer and Grünewald, he does not intrude his own personality or his passions. He "disappears behind his work," which is the greatest attribute of the portraitist. We sense the character of his people as we do those we meet in a sound novel, or better yet, in life. In addition there is the beauty of the pictures themselves, the adroit arrangement of the sitter with an eye to balance and composition, and the crystal clarity of line.

Like Jan van Eyck, Holbein was sent to foreign courts by his royal master to paint the pretty faces, if such could be found, of marriageable princesses. He visited four courts, in Flanders and France. The loveliest portrait he brought back was that of Christina of Denmark, Duchess of Milan, a possible wife for Henry, which was painted after a sitting of only three hours. But Christina declined the doubtful honor of becoming one of Henry's brides. ("Divorced, beheaded, died/Divorced, beheaded, survived" is the rhyme by which English schoolchildren remember the fates of Henry's wives.)

The next year Holbein journeyed to Cologne. There he painted Anne of Cleves, who was not pretty but did become Henry's wife, his fourth, but only for a few short months.

Holbein was one of the busiest men in London. He turned his hand to anything to make a living. He decorated the Steelyard, where the German colony gathered, arranged Anne Boleyn's coronation, and was in the middle of a painting of Henry with the Barber Surgeons when the Plague cut him off sharply. He was only forty-six.

Chapter 6
THE DUTCH PAINTERS

In 1609 the Dutch won a twelve years' truce from Spain. This divided the Netherlands very precisely into a Protestant north and a Catholic south. Flanders, the South, was still under the rule of Spain. This was the Flemish nation. Protestant Holland, the North, was a Republic. The cities of Amsterdam, Leyden, Haarlem, and The Hague were proud and free. Between 1609 and 1621 they sent more vessels to sea than England, Spain, and France combined. The people were vigorous, hard-working, well-to-do citizens. They liked pictures and could afford to buy them. But they disliked religious and historical pictures that brought up the Catholic past. What they wanted were Dutch themes, and Dutch faces; small paintings to hang in their neat Dutch homes, or large canvases that honored their big business and civic organizations. Rubens needed—and indeed had—palaces to paint. The Dutchman was content with a picture of his own backyard, or of his board of directors.

Frans Hals

c. 1580–1666

Frans Hals' pictures set you up. They make you feel that all's well with the world. They make you feel good. Hals himself felt good most of his life, though its end was long-drawn-out and sad.

He came of a strong-minded Protestant family of Haarlem, which was a stalwart city. For hundreds of years the sea had thundered against it, but Haarlem's bulwarks kept it back. The Spanish had only recently besieged it, but little Haarlem stood firm. Under

HALS. Self-portrait. Clowes Fund Collection, Indianapolis

HALS. Lady Governors of the Old Men's Home at Haarlem (*left*), and Officers of the Cluveniersdoelen (*right*). Frans Hals Museum, Haarlem.

their leader, William the Silent, 3000 men and 300 women, armed with muskets and daggers, held out against 30,000 fully equipped Spanish troops. After a seven months' siege, only 1600 of the defenders were left, and 12,000 of the besieging army had died of wounds and disease. Haarlemites were fearless and violently patriotic.

Hals was a hearty man, as can be seen from his jolly portrait of himself and his wife in their early, happier days, (see page 102). He was twenty-five when Holland won its independence, and it was after that that his career as an artist took hold. In a short time he was head of the largest guild of Haarlem painters.

To belong to a painters' guild at that time was the only way for an artist to make himself known. Artists no longer had rich patrons to finance them. They had to paint pictures that the public would buy. Twice a year the guilds held sales in which each member could display as many of his works as he liked. In this way Hals became enormously popular. He got commissions to paint military and civic groups and many single portraits. Haarlem is now a treasure house of these big, handsome group pictures.

Van Dyck, who was already in England, suggested that Hals join him, assuring him that King Charles would make it worth his while. But Frans declined the offer. Protestant that he was, Haarlemite, liberal, he preferred the plain easy-going society of his own people to the formality of a strange court.

Perhaps he was too easy-going. He had a wife and ten children to support, and although he was a hard worker and turned out many pictures, he enjoyed the tavern, and his best portraits—of singers, drinkers, musicians—indicate who were his chosen companions. As he grew old his popularity gradually dwindled, until in 1652, when he was sixty-eight, he was penniless. His creditors fell upon him—even the baker from whom he got his bread—and took everything he owned. It was little enough: three mattresses, a cupboard, a table, and six pictures.

The city of Haarlem granted him a small pension and three loads of peat yearly for fuel.

HALS. Portrait of Self and Wife (*right*) and detail (*left*). Rijksmuseum, Amsterdam.

HALS. The Laughing Cavalier. Reproduced by permission of the trustees of the Wallace Collection.

But his hand never lost its cunning. At the age of eighty he painted a group picture of the Lady Governors of the Old Men's Home at Haarlem (see page 101)—five elderly ladies in black silk dresses and white collars, each lady an individual. It is among his finest paintings. There was no longer a riot of color, but the feeling and the understanding is true gold.

He died a pauper, but the city of Haarlem built a museum outside its Almshouse where this painting and his other magnificent group pictures now hang.

Hals' portraits are unmistakable. He caught his sitter in action, laughing, gesturing, singing. Rubens, Rembrandt, and Velásquez posed their sitters in order to bring out certain characteristics, good or bad. But not Hals. This seeming casualness of his was accomplished only with the greatest care. In his earlier works the color was bright, and in his later years sober. Perhaps because by then he was painting the old and wrinkled, or possibly—as has been suggested—because the dark pigments were cheaper than the bright.

For two hundred years after his death Hals was almost forgotten. Then, in 1865 an Englishman rediscovered him and bought the *Laughing Cavalier* at an auction for 2040 pounds ($10,200). By 1908 the National Gallery of London paid 25,000 pounds for another Hals, and in 1960 still another sold for $509,600.

Jan Vermeer

1632–1675

It is hard to capture in words the exquisiteness of Jan Vermeer's gleaming genius. He is said never to have sold a picture in his lifetime, and after his death those of his pictures that were sold were under the name of the more popular artists of the day. It was 200 years before a Frenchman named Thoré discovered that here was one of the world's master painters.

Vermeer was born in Delft and lived there all his life in a house on the market square. This was also the studio where he painted. His father, an art dealer, left him his business when he died, and on this Jan supported his wife and nine children. That he did not support them in any luxury we know, because he left a painting on deposit with the baker to pay for bread, and when he died, his wife turned over another painting to his mother as security for a loan.

But it did leave the artist free to paint. One can see him in that studio which he so often put into his pictures, with its map, its tiled floor, its heavy drapery. How carefully he must have arranged his furniture, how exactly he placed the model! Nothing is hit-or-miss in the Vermeer canvas. The scene and its figures have been lovingly dwelt upon and studied, then executed with the impersonal, objective detachment of a Piero della Francesca or a Velásquez. The odd collection takes on a subtle harmony. The shapes and the spacing please. The tones of blue and the touch of lemon yellow, which he uses over and over again, are a delight. But most beautiful is the cool, clear shining light in which the whole is bathed—an inner radiance—which is one of the wonders of art.

Though Vermeer painted ordinary people in an ordinary room, this quality of light and color, this effect of space, this *completeness,* is his alone. A girl is standing beside a window. What the meaning of the picture is does not matter. She *is.* That is enough.

When he died at forty-three, Vermeer left fewer than forty pictures. It may be because he worked so painstakingly, therefore so slowly, that in his brief life there was time for no more. It may be because his pictures were not robust enough for the solid Dutch. At any rate he was soon forgotten, as was Hals. Twenty years after his death his pictures were sold for practically nothing. *The Kitchen Maid,* now in the famous Rijksmuseum in Amsterdam, went for 70 florins. When the museum bought it the price was 40,000 pounds (about $110,000).

VERMEER. The Artist in His Studio. Kunsthistorisches Museum, Vienna.

VERMEER. The Kitchen Maid. Rijksmuseum, Amsterdam.

TERBORCH. Curiosity. Metropolitan Museum of Art, New York. The Jules S. Bache Collection, 1949.

DE HOOCH. The Good Housewife. (*The Linen Closet*). Rijksmuseum, Amsterdam.

Far more popular with their contemporaries were the so-called "Little Dutchmen." The Dutch, as we said, loved their neat homes, their tiled floors, their well-brushed dogs and cats. They rated cleanliness so high that when a caller came to visit (so the story goes), the maid opened the door, picked him up in her arms, carried him to a chair, took off his boots so he would not soil the floor, and then announced him to the lady of the house.

It was these clean homes and the people who lived in them that the "Little Dutchmen" painted with such success. Like Jan van Eyck they checked on all objects in the scene and faithfully reproduced them. Like Bruegel they painted genre pictures—scenes from ordinary life.

Prominent among these painters were GERARD TERBORCH (1617–1681), PIETER DE HOOCH (1629–c. 1677), and JAN STEEN (1626–1679).

In Terborch's paintings the figures are small and precise, and the textures exquisite. In *Curiosity* it is the artist's sister, frequently his model, who leans over the letter writer.

In de Hooch the Dutch house comes into its own. *The Good Housewife* is typical—with the tiles, the closets, the shining woodwork, and neatness supreme.

JAN STEEN. The Merry Company, or As the Elders Sing. Gallery, The Hague.

At the top of this group was Jan Steen. Steen ran a brewery in Delft and an inn in Leyden, as painting apparently was not remunerative enough to keep his large boisterous family in comfort. He painted humorous scenes, witty and lightly satirical. (He always is laughing at them a bit himself.) He used his own family as models—his merry big wife, his in-laws, his children. He also painted the drunken, the boorish, the vulgar, the ugly that frequented his tavern, but all with such deftness that the homely subjects became symphonies of color.

Rembrandt

1606–1669

Rembrandt towers above all. He was one of the greatest painters that ever lived, and his paintings are among the best known in the world. You laughed with Bruegel, and had a sense of healthy well being with Frans Hals. Before Rembrandt you pause, and you think.

Rembrandt van Rijn was born at Leyden, the son of a well-to-do miller. He was one of five children and the only one that his parents saw fit to have educated. One brother became a baker, another a shoemaker, but Rembrandt was sent to the Latin School and the University. His heart, however, was not in his studies. It was in painting. In school and at home he sketched the faces of the people around him. He did at least eleven portraits of his father, and many beautiful ones of his mother. Even then the faces of the old fascinated him.

By the time he was twenty-five, Rembrandt was already launched on an artist's career and went to Amsterdam, then in its golden age and the commercial center of the world. It was a city made up of ring after ring of canals lined with fine buildings, but with none of the languor of Venice or the quaintness of Bruges;

REMBRANDT. The Polish Rider. The Frick Collection, New York.

105

REMBRANDT. Saskia as Flora. National
Gallery, London.

a big trading city with ships setting out for Persia, India, Japan,
and the West Indies—galleons, cockboats, and caravels. A hustling
city.

Rembrandt remained in Amsterdam for the rest of his life.
He is said never to have set foot out of Holland. He had no need
for Italy or England or Switzerland. The wide world of human
beings was his inspiration, and that he found on his doorstep.

His wife was the gentle Saskia, who appears in many of his
paintings, and he adored her. She had money of her own and
decked herself in jewels and beautiful clothes, probably to please
Rembrandt, who loved the textures of costumes, while he collected curios—Oriental capes, Asiatic carpets, helmets, swords—
many of which appear in his paintings. They lived in a fine
house, which is still standing, and they spent money extrav-
agantly. Rembrandt was Amsterdam's foremost painter. And for
eight years they were sublimely, thoughtlessly happy.

But at the end of those eight years his beloved Saskia died of
tuberculosis, leaving Rembrandt alone with their baby son, Titus.

His life now changed completely. It might have changed any-
way, for even before Saskia's death he was becoming increas-
ingly serious. He had already come to care less and less about

106

REMBRANDT. The Night Watch.
Rijksmuseum, Amsterdam.

what the public wanted, and more and more about his own painting ideals. Now he cut himself loose from the demands of the
world and painted as he pleased. *The Night Watch* is an example
of his complete independence. It was commissioned by members
of the Civic Guard, but instead of the customary row of exact
portraits that the members assumed they were paying for, Rembrandt painted a scene of darkness and light, of mystery and
romance, of figures caught at a dramatic moment, many of them
indistinguishable among the shadows. This definitely was not
what the officials wanted.

He now moved into a house in the Jewish section of Amsterdam. Holland had given shelter to the Jews expelled from
Spain, and this ancient race, with the story of suffering written
on the faces of the old, appealed to the artist. He painted many
Jews into his famous Bible illustrations.

The Bible illustrations were etchings. Etching differs from engraving in that the artist does not draw directly on the copper
plate. Instead, he covers the plate with a protective substance
and draws upon that with a needle. Then the plate is put into
acid. Where the needle has scratched away the substance, the
picture is etched. Then the plate is inked and the etching is re-

107

REMBRANDT. Christ Healing the Sick, (the "Hundred-Guilder Print"), etching.

produced on paper. Rembrandt's etchings are among the finest in the world. Nowhere is his conception of Christ more touching than in his etching known as the "Hundred-Guilder Print."

During these years Hendrickje, who had been Saskia's maid, lived with him as faithful housekeeper and model. She could not read or write, but to the end of her days she took care of the artist and the growing Titus. She left Rembrandt free to paint, and painting filled his life. Unlike Hals he was not convivial; he disliked small talk and casual comradeship. What was more important, he never tried to make connections with persons of importance, so that by 1656 he had seventy-two pictures piled up in his house unsold.

REMBRANDT. Portrait of Hendrickje Stoffels. The Louvre, Paris.

108

Then the world caught up with him. He had long since spent the money left him by Saskia, and fourteen years after her death his creditors seized his house, his curios, his paintings. They threw everything together on the street—pictures, saucepans, chairs, shoes; and, to the great man's deep humiliation, sold them, before his eyes, at a quarter of their value. Among those who executed the bankruptcy proceedings were four men who had been painted by him in *The Night Watch*. (In the light of his poverty-stricken years, it is ironic that one of Rembrandt's paintings, *Aristotle Contemplating the Bust of Homer*, was bought by the Metropolitan Museum of Art, New York, in 1961, for $2,300,000, the largest amount ever paid for any painting.)

But Rembrandt went on undaunted. Hendrickje had hidden some etchings which she now sold and the three of them moved into a still poorer corner of the ghetto. Rembrandt had been allowed to keep his painting equipment, and continued to paint—even more magnificently. His mind was occupied with visions, and the present, however uncomfortable, made little impression. Titus stayed with him, and Rembrandt worshiped him, and painted him over and over again.

Rembrandt was the supreme artist of chiaroscuro—of transparent shadows and the blending of light and shade. Whereas Raphael, for instance, painted everything in full light, Rembrandt's figures shine out against the darkness. Raphael's outlines are sharply defined, Rembrandt's merge with the background. His colors are dark browns, grays, black, with a rich yellow for contrast. His paintings are totally unlike the work of any other painter.

REMBRANDT. Aristotle Contemplating the Bust of Homer. The Metropolitan Museum of Art, New York, purchased with special funds and gifts of friends of the Museum, 1961.

109

The Pilgrims of Emmaus is one of his finest works. Rembrandt was a Protestant and deeply religious in a personal way. All his life he thought about the man that Jesus was, and year after year, in drawings, etchings, and paintings, he sought to portray that love of mankind which he believed to be the essence of Christ. He did 145 paintings, and more than 650 drawings and etchings on Biblical subjects.

He has left many versions of the Emmaus story. In this picture, Christ, at the inn, has just been recognized. The three men are looking at him with astonishment and awe. He has endured tortures. He has passed through death. His halo surrounds him with an unearthly glow, yet he is very gentle and very human. He is humble, ready to help and to pity.

REMBRANDT. The Pilgrims of Emmaus.
The Louvre, Paris.

In his understanding of human beings Rembrandt is often compared to Shakespeare. He dedicated his life to portraying the best and the deepest of man's nature. It was the soul of man, not his appearance, that interested him. Nowhere do we see this so well as in the last of his many self-portraits. (Throughout his life he did nearly one hundred self-portraits, never for vanity, but to put into paint exactly what he saw revealed.) Now Titus had died, like his mother, of tuberculosis; Hendrickje had died; and Rembrandt was alone in the rags of poverty. But there is no self-pity in this wide wrinkled face. Only the serenity of a free conscience, of life's difficulties overcome—the blessed relief of an artist who knows that he has not worked in vain.

REMBRANDT. Self-portrait at Advanced Age. National Gallery, London.

Chapter 7
THE SPANISH PAINTERS

Spain was the most powerful country in Europe in the late sixteenth century. She had conquered Portugal, she ruled Flanders. Her adventurous explorers had discovered the New World from which came vast quantities of gold. Through the eyes of Bruegel we have seen how her soldiers terrified the Flemish. And we know from our own histories the ruthlessness and cruelty of some of the *conquistadors* in Mexico and Peru.

Spain was a land of contrasts. Her nobles lived in palatial magnificence, all others in direst poverty. The Spanish court was notoriously extravagant, its courtiers indolent and without ambition. The energetic Moors had already been expelled, and the Jews had fled the iron hand of the Inquisition. But many Moors and Jews, converted to Catholicism, remained, and their blood mingled with the Castilian and the Asturian and the Andalusian Spanish.

The Protestant Reformation in Germany brought on the Counter Reformation in Spain. This was a rekindling of religious feeling, a return to the mysticism and spirituality of the Middle Ages, which had a pronounced influence on art. The two new art forms inspired by the Counter Reformation were the Baroque, which came to full bloom in Rubens, and Mannerism. The supreme Mannerist painter was El Greco.

EL GRECO. Portrait of a Man (perhaps the artist). Metropolitan Museum of Art, New York, Purchase, 1924, Joseph Pulitzer Bequest.

EL GRECO. View of Toledo. Metropolitan Museum of Art, New York, Bequest of Mrs. H. O. Havemeyer, 1929. The H. O. Havemeyer Collection.

El Greco

c. 1541–1614

Even to modern eyes accustomed to shocks in art, El Greco seems infinitely strange. His elongated figures with their dead white faces and deep-set eyes have a look of madness. We find him hard to understand. Yet in his own time he was accepted and admired.

He was born Domenicos Theotocopoulos, on the island of Crete, which at that time belonged to Greece—hence the name by which he came to be known, El Greco, "the Greek." He lived on Crete until he was about twenty-five, then left it to see the world, and never returned. But he always chose to remain Greek, and signed his name to his pictures with Greek characters.

His first port of call was Venice. Up to now the young man from Crete had seen only stiff Byzantine-Greek religious paintings, and the art of Venice, then at its height, intoxicated him with the ease of its figures and the beauty of the color. Some believe that he studied with Titian, then the great master of Venice. But Tintoretto, with his feverish new style, seemed to make a stronger impression.

From Venice El Greco went to Rome. But the order and harmony of true Renaissance art left him cold.

At thirty-four he moved on to Spain and there discovered the perfect spot for his particular genius, Toledo, the mysterious romantic city high on the banks of the Tagus River, dark gray

113

EL GRECO. The Virgin with Saint Ines and Saint Tecla. Widener Collection, National Gallery of Art, Washington, D.C.

beneath greenish clouds, a city of mosques and synagogues and convents, Christian, Moorish, Jewish, the home at that time of St. Theresa of Avila and of Cervantes, author of *Don Quixote*. Here El Greco settled down and lived in great content for the rest of his life. (His painting of Toledo, see page 113, is said to be the most popular picture in the Metropolitan Museum of Art in New York.)

El Greco created a style of painting all his own, but one which was well suited to the Spanish temperament. He painted a mystical view of the world. His figures yearn toward heaven. Their heads, outlined in misty light, are divine. The garments, the clouds, the gesturing hands move with rhythm. Everything is caught in spiritual rapture. Everything spirals upward and onward. Caravaggio had painted saints as real people. El Greco painted them in the mysteriousness of their religious fervor. Even his portraits are unreal—emaciated people, wasted away by their emotions.

This is pure Mannerist art.

Mannerist art had its start in Rome. The Reformation did not touch the Catholic Church in Italy or Spain. But the restlessness it aroused throughout Europe had an effect upon the art of those countries. A reaction set in against the confidence which man had in himself during the High Renaissance, well exemplified in Raphael. Artists began to picture man as frenzied and tortured. Even Michelangelo's later figures were contorted, and the artists who followed him tried to outdo the master in twistings and writhings. They painted "in the manner of," which gave name to this style. For them there was no beauty without strangeness, a certain artificiality, and a suggestion of the neurotic. After the calm of the High Renaissance their art seems restless and disturbed.

El Greco was a strange man himself. Once an artist friend called on him. It was a bright sunny day. But El Greco sat alone in his house in a darkened room, neither working nor sleeping. When his friend urged him to come out, he refused: the light of day, he said, would disturb the light shining within himself.

He painted with fiery imagination, but he had himself well in hand. Everything was thought through. He was sure of himself and accepted none of the teachings of other artists. For him color was far more important than drawing, and Michelangelo, the draughtsman, according to El Greco, did not know how to paint. He demanded high prices for his paintings and went to court if he did not get them. He loved lawsuits.

El Greco's household in Toledo was a happy one. The beautiful dark-eyed woman who appears in so many of his works was the mother of his son, and the son was the center of his father's universe. They lived in splendor in a twenty-four-room house, with a fine library of Greek and Roman books, and musicians to play for them at meals.

During his lifetime El Greco was highly successful. He painted for King Philip II, for the grandees, and the high churchmen. But almost at once after his death a new wave swept over the

EL GRECO. The Vision of St. John.
Metropolitan Museum of Art, New York,
Rogers Fund.

world of art. Velásquez became court painter and introduced an entirely new painting technique. Rubens came to Spain from Flanders with his robust love of life. And the Baroque was in.

El Greco was soon forgotten. Not until the Expressionists in Germany and the "Fauves" in France rediscovered him in the twentieth century, did he again come into his own. Nearly three hundred years after his death the spirit of El Greco was revived in the paintings of Vincent Van Gogh, Gauguin and even Picasso.

Because El Greco was not popular during the nineteenth century when Europeans were building up their art collections, Americans, who began collecting somewhat later, were able to acquire more El Grecos than collectors in any other country except Spain itself. There are seven El Grecos in the Metropolitan Museum in New York alone.

115

VELÁSQUEZ. Portrait of Philip IV.
National Gallery, London.

Diego Velásquez

1599–1660

Spain had begun to decline.

During the 400 years that the Moors had lived in Spain, they had made it a fertile garden. They were agricultural experts. But Philip II had expelled the Moors, and by the time his grandson Philip IV came to power the irrigation system that the Moors had built had gone to pieces, crops were miserable, and the people were hungry. The enterprising Jews were gone. The Armada had been defeated off the coast of England in 1588. And the English and the French had pushed their way into the rich new world of America.

Philip IV sat helpless on his throne watching his country grow weaker, and his own power drain away. All he enjoyed was his horses, and he escaped to them when he could. Court life was dismally formal. Dwarfs and clowns and degenerates were brought in to try to amuse the bored courtiers. Clothes were stiff with hoops and bones and starch. No one could relax.

For forty-five years Philip's power continued to dwindle, and for thirty-seven of those years Velásquez painted him—from the not very confident youth with his dogs to the patient long-enduring elderly man. Velásquez was Philip's court painter and his dearly beloved friend.

Such was Velásquez's world—the king, his family, and their retainers. It would be hard to find anywhere in history a less attractive group. But out of them came some of the finest painting ever known.

Diego Rodriguez de Silva y Velásquez was born in Seville. He was the son of a lawyer, but his heart was in painting. He studied under Pacheco, who was not a very good teacher, but had a lovely daughter, Juana, with whom the young man fell in love. They married before he was quite nineteen.

Velásquez's own family belonged to the small nobility, which was always a matter of pride to Diego. His appointment as court painter in Madrid at the age of twenty-four was a still greater satisfaction. And when he visited Italy, even though he was already a well-known painter, he chose to be received not as an artist, but as a friend of the King of Spain. Yet his status at court was much the same as that of the dwarfs and degenerates. He had a studio in the palace rent-free, he and his family received presents of wine and food from the royal kitchen, and he wore the king's cast-off clothes. He was not allowed to sell any pictures, but had to paint only on the king's orders.

It was Rubens, on one of his visits to Madrid, who persuaded Philip to send Velásquez to Italy in order that he might study the works of the Italian masters.

Velásquez went twice to Italy. He was very much impressed with Venetian painting but was heard to tell a fellow artist that Raphael pleased him not at all.

116

VELÁSQUEZ. Portrait of Philip IV. The Prado, Madrid.

Like El Greco he had moved a long way from the Raphael-
ian symmetry and orderliness of the High Renaissance, but in
a different direction. His court paintings have the grandeur of
the Baroque—the sweep of sky and cloud and prancing horse,
in the early painting of the King, and the princeliness of all the
portraits.

Where the Flemish and Dutch artists painted every hair and
every petal, Velásquez got a rich effect with spots of color,
patches of light. He painted "what the eye sees"—the light and
air between the eye and the object.

As a painter he was impersonal and detached. So were Piero
della Francesca and Vermeer. When we stand before a painting of any of these artists it is as if a veil were removed and the
figures were revealed. As if they had been existing there for all
eternity.

Unlike Rembrandt, who was interested in man's soul, Velásquez was interested in the King, the dwarf, the Infanta—only

117

VELÁSQUEZ. The Maids of Honor.
The Prado, Madrid.

118

VELÁSQUEZ. The Dwarf, Don Sebastian de Morra. The Prado, Madrid.

VELÁSQUEZ. Pope Innocent X (detail of head). Doria Palace, Rome.

as objects to be painted. He never flattered his sitters, as Van Dyck did, nor idealized them, as Titian did his dreamy young men. Yet he revealed the depths of their beings. The dwarf has dignity. He understands what his deformity means in his relation to the world. This understanding lies in his eyes, as it does in the eyes of the sad, inactive old king. Probably no painter has ever expressed so completely the hopeless misery of man alone, with no one to turn to but himself.

In his famous picture *The Maids of Honor* we see the little Princess Margarita with her friends, the artist himself at the side painting, and in a mirror at the back the reflection of the child's mother and father, the King and Queen. We, the spectators, are there too—in the room—not outside looking at a picture. This is also strictly Baroque. The Red Cross of Santiago in this picture was said to have been painted on the artist's breast by the King himself. In order to receive this high honor it had to be proven through many generations that his lineage was pure: no taint of Moorish or Jewish blood, and no contamination by trade.

Velásquez's pictures present what we would call reality. But his manner of achieving reality was an entirely new technique. He did not draw figures and objects in outline. He suggested them, and left our imaginations to fill them out, as can be seen in the mirrored reflection. As someone said of his portrait of the Pope, "It is made out of nothing—yet there it is!"

The French Impressionists, nearly three hundred years later, "discovered" Velásquez. Renoir wept in front of the picture of the princess. "The whole painting lies in the little pink bow!"

Velásquez died suddenly of a fever in 1660, and his wife, Juana, died eight days later. The church in which they were buried was destroyed by Napoleon's troops in 1811, and no one knows now where the great painter lies.

GOYA. Self-portrait. Collection of the
Smith College Museum of Art, North-
ampton, Massachusetts.

Francisco Goya

1746–1828

Goya was born the poorest of the poor, and became the most
famous man in Spain. He was a notorious adventurer, yet the
King made him court painter.

He was born Francisco Goya y Lucientes, in a stone hut in the
bleak mountain section of Spain. He worked with his brother in the
fields, until, as the story goes, the village priest saw him drawing
with charcoal on a wall. Whether this Giotto-esque story is true or
not, he did get a chance at the age of twelve to paint a curtain of
the village church. This started him off on an artist's career and he
was sent to Saragossa to study painting.

But city life went to the boy's head. He became what we
would now call a juvenile delinquent—a teen-age gangster. After
one bitter battle between rival gangs, three boys were found
dead, and Goya departed for Madrid.

In Madrid his companions were bull fighters, gypsies, gamblers.
He had a fine voice and danced a lively step, and was a great

120

favorite with the girls. But gang wars continued and one morning Goya was found in a gutter with a dagger in his back. He survived and was quietly sent out of the country till things settled down.

Once back in Madrid he married and had twenty children. All of them were sickly, and only one lived to grow up, but each in his turn was beloved. Goya's pictures of children are among the best in the world.

He continued to be a roisterer, but now with a higher class of society. He was made court painter by Charles IV; and the Duchess of Alba, a famous beauty, made him her favorite. He used her as model for some of his finest pictures and he painted the decadent court in all its terrible truth.

Goya stood in awe of no one. In his paintings royalty looks "like the grocer's family that has just won a big lottery prize." He never flattered. He could make the King a moron, and the Queen unbelievably evil—the truth in both cases—with neither aware of the pointing finger. The uglier his people, the better he painted them. They are all intensely vivid and indisputably Spanish. Four generations of Spanish rulers, as well as all the most famous men and women of his day, were at the mercy of Goya's ruthless brush.

He came to manhood in a time of revolution. He lived through the days of the French Revolution and of Napoleon. He saw the whole of Europe fighting for freedom.

GOYA. The Duchess of Alba. The Hispanic Society of America, New York.

GOYA. The Royal Family of Charles IV. The Prado, Madrid.

GOYA. Don Manuel Osorio de Zuniga.
Metropolitan Museum of Art, New York,
Jules S. Bache Collection.

GOYA. The Third of May, 1808.
The Prado, Madrid.

One of his most famous works is *The Third of May*. This was the tragic day when Napoleon's army entered Madrid and Murat's firing squad slaughtered the people. The story is that Goya came upon the scene the morning after, and on this historic occasion— as once long before—he again painted on a wall. He dipped his handkerchief in the blood of the corpses still lying there and sketched the composition with their blood on the wall beside them. True or not, nowhere in art is war more fearful than in this magnificent painting of terrified unarmed citizens facing soldiers with pointed guns.

Goya was a rebel, but not necessarily a patriot. When France took over the rule of Spain, he worked for King Joseph Bonaparte, and after Bonaparte's downfall had to go in hiding for three months to escape the wrath of the Spaniards.

At seventy-eight he was nearly blind. He had been totally deaf since he was forty-six, yet he crossed the Pyrenees mountains alone into France and proceeded to the city of Bordeaux, still tough and still painting. There he died in his eighty-third year.

More than any other single painter Goya inspired the painting of the late nineteenth century in France. In his anger, in his reality, his concentration on the life around him, he had a powerful influence on the artists soon to follow—on Delacroix, Daumier, Courbet, and Manet.

123

PART TWO
MODERN ART

★   ★   ★

Chapter 8

THE BRIDGE
FROM THE OLD MASTERS
TO MODERN ART

The eighteenth century and the first half of the nineteenth was a period of interlude. For three centuries genius had followed genius in a brilliant pageant that ended with a final burst of energy in the canvases of Rubens in the north and Velásquez in Spain. Then the spirit flagged. Not until the middle of the nineteenth century did great art come to flower again. In Paris in the 1860s a group of earnest painters once more appeared. They caused an epoch-making upheaval which we now recognize as one of the most creative periods in the entire history of art. But this magnificent blooming did not happen overnight—nor entirely of itself. Throughout that long, somewhat stagnant, century and a half, new influences crept in, smaller painters led the way to new techniques. Above all, great social changes occurred in the life of Europeans.

BOURBON FRANCE

Our scene shifts to France.

Under the long reign of Louis XIV, from 1643 to 1715, France succeeded Spain as the predominant power in Europe. Louis XIV, the "Sun King," made himself the supreme dictator. *"L'Etat, c'est moi!"* (The State, it is I!) was his slogan.

To set off his magnificence before the world, Louis built Versailles, an enormous palace a few miles from Paris surrounded by miles of formal park—a mighty mass of galleries, wings, halls, courts, apartments, huge rooms, high ceilings, arches, mirrored walls, with more than a hundred windows looking out over lawns, trees, shrubbery, statues, fountains, paths. Against this dramatic royal background, Louis assembled his family, his staff, his courtiers, his world; 5000 persons lived under the palace roof, 2000 horses champed in the stables, 3000 to 4000 servants in gorgeous livery stood passively by, waiting to pick up a handkerchief or pass a silver tray.

POUSSIN. Shepherds of Arcady (Et in Arcadia Ego). The Louvre, Paris.

But life was not gay under the watchful eye of the Sun King. The court was dull and pompous. And art tended to be the same. In order to keep artists as well as courtiers in hand, Louis founded the French Royal Academy, designed to guide them in the paths of strict artistic respectability. A little Venetian color, a little Rubens movement, and considerable classical elegance was the formula, as exemplified in the work of NICOLAS POUSSIN (1594–1665), its head.

When Louis XIV died in 1715, after more than a half century of heavy-handed supremacy, France breathed a sigh of relief. Courtiers moved to Paris and built elegant small palaces of their own, painters were called in to decorate them, art turned to love and ladies. This new style was called Rococo. It was a lighthearted

WATTEAU. Embarkation for Cythera. The Louvre, Paris.

outgrowth of the Baroque. Where the lines in Louis's day had been straight, they now curved. Where furniture had been solid, it was now delicate. Ornaments that had been heavy became airy. The spirit of solemnity changed to the light breezes of fun and frivolity. Ladies applied rouge, powder, and patches to add to their beauty. Men wore embroidered waistcoats, diamond rosettes on their shoes, cascades of lace at their cuffs.

ANTOINE WATTEAU (1684–1721) was the Rococo painter *par excellence*. His was a dreamy world of gallant cavaliers, pretty ladies in gleaming silks, woodland landscapes with lacy trees, picnics, swings, and love. Giorgione had the same touch, but Giorgione's turned to poetry, while Watteau's remained wistful and lightly sportive.

In Watteau's paintings this rather subtle note of sadness reflects his own hopelessness. For many years he was ill with tuberculosis, for which there was no cure in those days. Death was always around the corner, and carried him off when he was only thirty-seven. As an artist he was hypersensitive; forever dissatisfied with what he produced, and sure that he was overpaid.

Watteau captured the spirit of the Rococo, which maintained its lighthearted sway for most of the century. Its goddess was Marie Antoinette, Queen of France, whose frivolities led from enormous hats to a make-believe rustic village she had built in Versailles. It was the extravagance of the nobility in these butterfly days that started intelligent men thinking and incited the impoverished and the undernourished to slowly rising anger. The artificialities of the Rococo world soon gave way to the Age of Reason.

ENGLAND AND THE AGE OF REASON

Nowhere do we see the Age of Reason in action so well as in eighteenth-century England—sturdy, prosperous, plain. England had no flamboyant Baroque, and she now had no Rococo. Her contribution to art lay in literature rather than in painting. Samuel Johnson was compiling his dictionary. Oliver Goldsmith was writing *The Vicar of Wakefield*. Sheridan was writing plays. Where France was divided into frivolous aristocrats and downtrodden poor, England was developing a strong middle class.

The only way an English painter could make a living in the eighteenth century was by painting portraits. Portraits had always been popular. Holbein, as we have seen, had come from Germany to paint the robust, well-fed figures of Henry VIII's court in the sixteenth century. In the seventeenth century Van Dyck depicted the court of Charles I, paler, more slender, more elegant, and more aristocratic than they really were. Now two rival English portrait painters took the fashionable world by storm.

THOMAS GAINSBOROUGH (1727–1788) was only a little less popular than his rival JOSHUA REYNOLDS (1723–1792). Gainsborough painted only 1000 to Reynolds' 2000. Actually Gainsborough preferred to paint landscapes, which would not sell; and

GAINSBOROUGH. Mary, Countess of Howe. Kenwood House, London.

127

REYNOLDS. Portrait of Captain Robert Orme. National Gallery, London.

would rather have walked in the country or played his viola da gamba, than paint at all. Reynolds' paintings tended to be somewhat labored beside the lightness and effortlessness of his rival's. But both were known to the art world as "face painters"—"portrait manufacturers."

Against what seemed to them social pandering by the portraitists, two English artists, Hogarth and Blake, stood forth in open rebellion. In the history of art, rebels are likely to get more notice but fewer orders, and such was the case with these two.

WILLIAM HOGARTH (1697–1764), indisputably a man of the Age of Reason, looked down on the fashionable in art. He was a good painter as we see in his famous painting, *The Graham Children*. But he had to try another medium to catch the public. Having studied the work of Jan Steen, the "Little Dutchman" who specialized in humorous home scenes, Hogarth now undertook a series

HOGARTH. The Graham Children. Tate Gallery, London.

of episodes drawn from London life. *The Rake's Progress* was one of these series of moral lessons, humorous on the surface but severely sober in their protest against injustice, especially against the cruelty rampant in English prisons and insane asylums. (The Rake, in his downhill journey from frivolity to crime to disease to madness, finally reaches the bottom in Bedlam, the insane asylum.) Hogarth once said that he would rather put an end to cruelty than be the creator of Raphael's greatest pictures.

These series he made into engravings, and unlike his paintings they sold as fast as he made them. People were willing to pay for thrills.

HOGARTH. The Rake in Bedlam, engraving.

129

BLAKE. Ezekiel's Vison, watercolor.
Museum of Fine Arts, Boston.

WILLIAM BLAKE (1757–1827), on the other hand, turned his back on life itself and escaped into a world of visions. At the age of four he imagined he saw God. Somewhat later he saw a flock of angels sitting in a tree. These visions he put both into poetry and onto canvas. That the public had no interest whatsoever in his paintings did not bother him. "I wish to do nothing for money," he said. "I wish to live for art." This was his philosophy and his practice. He never could make a living, died in poverty, and was buried in a pauper's grave. But he died singing hallelujahs. His wife, Kate, whom other artists called "the perfect wife," stood by him faithfully to the end.

His paintings were fantastic. Once a Blake painting was shown to King George III. "Take it away!" he screamed.

The people of his day thought Blake mad. His mystical vision bewildered them. "To see the world in a grain of sand/And a heaven in a wild flower,/Hold infinity in the palm of your hand, /And eternity in an hour." He was what we now call a symbolist, a painter whose figures, objects, and scenes represent not reality, but ideas; and his influence on the art of today is probably greater than that of any other English painter.

English landscapists were also breaking new ground.

JOHN CONSTABLE (1776–1837) painted the green of England that Wordsworth and Coleridge and Keats put into their poetry. He painted only landscapes, and only the landscapes of his home county, Suffolk. He was among the first artists to paint outdoors,

CONSTABLE. The Hay Wain. National Gallery, London.

TURNER. The Fighting Téméraire.
Tate Gallery, London.

the better to observe the changes of light and color in nature. He
was what we would now call a "realist" (one who aims to represent
things as they really are)—a forerunner of the still unborn Impressionists. But in order to make his pictures saleable he gave in
to the public, and frequently painted two versions of the same
scene, one for himself—nature as he saw it—the other to exhibit,
with the shiny finish and the dark colors then prevalent.

He was a modest, quiet man who never made himself conspicu-
ous, but his influence on art immediately to follow was profound.
"Painting for me is but another word for feeling," he said, which
was a long cry from the prevalent attitude in the French academic
circles. When his landscape *The Hay Wain* hung in the Paris
Salon of 1824, a young French painter named Delacroix hailed
Constable as a great new master.

WILLIAM TURNER (1775–1851) went still further along the
path toward modern art. He was a strange figure—a child prodigy
who exhibited a painting in the Royal Academy in London at the

131

TURNER. The Snowstorm. National Gallery, London.

age of fifteen. He was the son of a Cockney barber, remained a Cockney all his life, and was always conscious of his lowly birth and oppressed by it.

Where Constable painted a patch of Suffolk over and over again, Turner painted the world. He visited Italy, reveled in Venice, and walked twenty-five miles a day in the British Isles. Once he joined a fishing fleet bound for the North Sea, and during a storm tied himself to the mast in order to miss no detail.

Everything in the natural world was subject for his brush—the sky, the clouds, the mist, the rain, the river and the raging sea, fire, water, steam. Above all he worshiped the sun. His is nature at its greatest. He fused the elements till form all but disappeared in the fervor of luminous color.

Once a woman was watching him paint outdoors. "I don't see it the way you do!" she said severely.

"Don't you wish you did!" answered Turner.

But two French artists, thirty years later, fleeing to London to escape the Franco-Prussian War, saw what Turner saw. They were overwhelmed by his brilliant technique and later introduced it to France, thus opening a new chapter in the history of art. They were Monet and Pissarro, the first Impressionists.

Turner amassed a fortune from his paintings. People bought his paintings because, unlike gentle Constable's, they were dramatic and exciting. He left 19,000! But like Michelangelo, in spite of his worldly success he lived alone in miserable surroundings and, like Michelangelo, worked day and night without help. No one knew where he lived. Few ever saw him paint. And he died in unnecessary squalor.

COUNTER REVOLUTION

The French Revolution changed the course of life throughout Europe. The life of elegance gave way to the Reign of Terror. Gone were the picnics and the pretty ladies. The nobility lost prestige and property, the working man came into his own. It was a political and social upheaval, the effects of which remain with us today.

In art, however, the revolutionary effects were reversed. Painters, instead of gaining freedom, lost it.

The leading painter of the French Revolution was JACQUES LOUIS DAVID (1748–1825), known as the guillotine artist. He was one of the committee that sentenced Louis XVI to die; and standing on the side lines as the tumbril passed, he sketched Marie Antoinette, wife of Louis, on her way to her execution.

He was an agile politician. When Robespierre, the Terrorist, was assassinated and the Revolution collapsed, when Napoleon stepped to the front and took over, David became Napoleon's man. Both of them are identified with what is called Neo-Classicism. Pompeii and Herculaneum, buried deep under the lava of Mount Vesuvius for centuries, had recently been excavated, and the late Roman style discovered there became the latest in French fashion. Furniture, ornamentation, ladies' gowns, painting, all became severely classical. This new art did not capture the beauty of ancient art, it only copied it in a coldly distant, intellectual way. But it dominated the Empire.

As Napoleon took over the country, David took over the dictatorship of art. He abolished the Academy of Louis XIV and substituted the Institute of France. According to the dictates of the Institute, art must be "noble"; painters must choose their subjects

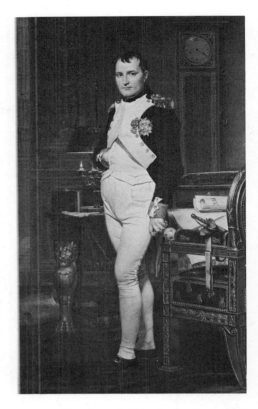

DAVID. Napoleon in His Study. Samuel H. Kress Collection, National Gallery of Art, Washington, D.C.

DAVID. The Death of Socrates. Metropolitan Museum of Art, New York, Wolfe Fund, 1931.

INGRES. Mme. Moitessier Seated. National
Gallery, London.

from mythology; story and moral must be emphasized; drawing,
not color, was all important.

The Academy of Fine Arts was a section of the Institute of
France, and its power over art throughout most of the nineteenth
century was formidable. It chose the teachers of the official art
school (Ecole des Beaux Arts) and the directors of the French
Academy in Rome. Twice a year it sponsored a show of artists'
work in Paris, known as the Salon. The paintings hung in the
Salon were chosen by a jury controlled by the Academy, and no
artist turned down by this jury could get his pictures before the
public. Pictures for museums and for the Emperor himself, orders
for murals in public buildings—all were selected through the Di-
rector of Fine Arts, who in turn was under the influence of the
Academy. Every new movement in art was suppressed. And the
public, fearful of being wrong, followed blindly.

David's successor as head of the Institute and supreme dictator
of Neo-Classicism, was his pupil JEAN AUGUSTE DOMINIQUE
INGRES (1780–1867). There was nothing revolutionary in Ingres's
nature, and his influence on art was ultraconservative. He was a
draughtsman first, a painter second. "Anything that is well drawn
is well enough painted," he said. And under him the Academy
began to turn out paintings that were precise, colorless, and cold.

134

His own elegant pencil portraits became very famous, and his painting—even though he decried color—was of a beautiful subtlety which his own followers never quite grasped.

At the opposite pole from Ingres was his lifelong enemy in art, EUGÈNE DELACROIX (1798–1863). Delacroix was a Romanticist. "Who will deliver us from the Greeks and Romans?" asked the Romanticists. They were the first rebels against art dictatorship and the Academicians. They were anti-David, anti-Ingres, anti-Napoleon. They reveled in Rubens and the Venetians, in vivid color, dramatic lighting, excitement. The poet Byron was their hero.

Delacroix was the Romanticist supreme: tall, slender, and frail, a highly intelligent, restless, and imaginative man. Always elegantly tailored and considered the best conversationalist in Paris, he spent his evenings in the company of countesses. Some say he was the son of Talleyrand.

His paintings were on the sketchy side. As part of his rebellion against Ingres, he chose to be careless in drawing. His color was brilliant, and the swing of his pictures feverishly exciting. As someone said, Delacroix could make a battle painting look like a bouquet of flowers.

This wild recklessness brought about a new kind of revolution. The Institute of France continued to exist, and its members insulted Delacroix to the end of his life. But today Delacroix is regarded by the French as the father of modern French art. He freed color and opened the way for the Impressionists.

DELACROIX. Arab Attacked by a Lion. The Art Institute of Chicago, Chicago, Potter Palmer Collection.

135

The next deviation from the Academicians was "the return to nature." A group of artists went out to the village of Barbizon on the outskirts of the Forest of Fontainebleau, not only because it was cheaper and quieter than Paris, but because it was close to nature. Only in nature, they believed, could man find the divine.

JEAN FRANÇOIS MILLET (1814–1875) painted humble peasants at work in the fields. He painted them because he knew and loved them, not because he considered them downtrodden. He was not a propaganda painter. But the Salon promptly rejected his pictures. "Why," they asked, "should we hang the paintings of a man who doesn't change his linen?"

JEAN BAPTISTE CAMILLE COROT (1796–1875) was a simple-hearted generous painter who lived and painted happily close to nature for eighty years. Not until he was fifty did he get official recognition, and during all those years his father heartily disapproved of him. But when he received the Légion d'honneur for one of his pictures, his father had a change of heart. "He must have some talent!" his father exclaimed, which typifies the general atti-

MILLET. The Gleaners. The Louvre, Paris.

tude of the public toward artists. If officially approved, they must be good.

During his own day Corot was best known for his misty landscapes with fuzzy trees. But his figure paintings, strong and realistic, are far better, and at long last have become popular with the buying public.

GUSTAVE COURBET (1819–1877) went one step further than the Barbizon painters in regard to nature. "It is better to paint dunghills," he said, "than not to paint nature at all." He is known as a Realist. He painted poor people not, like Millet, because he loved them, but becaust they *were* downtrodden. He opened the floodgates and released the "common man." He spurned everything that was fanciful, religious, or romantic. When, in 1855, the official Academy rejected his paintings for the annual Salon show, he built himself a pavilion, hung his own pictures in it, and called it Pavilion of Realism. He went on record as a socialist. He painted himself in working clothes and called his picture *Bon*

137

COROT. The Sibyl. Metropolitan Museum of Art, New York, Bequest of Mrs. H. O. Havemeyer, 1929. H. O. Havemeyer Collection.

GUSTAVE COURBET. Bon Jour, M. Courbet.
Musée Fabre, Montpellier.

Jour, M. Courbet. His desire was to shock people into recognition of what was wrong with the world. "Courbet," said the writer Zola, "has democratic indigestion."

HONORÉ DAUMIER (1808–1879) was another realist who, like Millet and Courbet, looked closely at the world about him. Though he was a good painter he never submitted a picture to the Salon. He made a living drawing cartoons for a Paris paper, as long as the paper would keep him. In his cartoons he caricatured the exorbitant tax collector, the unworthy lawyer, the foolish complacent bourgeois. He had the deepest compassion for the poor and the oppressed, and nothing but ridicule for the pretentious.

"This boy has something of Michelangelo in him," said the novelist Balzac, who worked on the same paper. Delacroix and Courbet and Corot used to visit him in his little flat in the oldest part of Paris. They would sit on the floor smoking, discussing art and life, the three visitors conscious that the greatest artist among them was Daumier. Yet he would have starved when the paper let him go had it not been for his friends. Nearly blind, he moved to the country into a small house that Corot had quietly bought for him. There he died, alone and penniless.

The Salon could not have cared less.

138

DAUMIER. The Third-Class Carriage.
Metropolitan Museum of Art, New York,
Bequest of Mrs. H. O. Havemeyer, 1929.
H. O. Havemeyer Collection.

139

DAUMIER. A Good Argument. The Fogg
Art Museum, Cambridge.

THE SALON

In the old days men of wealth were deeply concerned with art. They appreciated the artist, took him into their palaces to live, gave him walls to paint, and put the power of their influence behind him. But in the nineteenth century all that was changed.

A new kind of society grew up. Poor people were moving in from the farms to find work in the cities, and the cities became overcrowded, dirty, and grimey. The working man at the machine took the place of the man who had worked with his hands. A middle class came into existence, among whom were rich powerful industrialists.

These new men of wealth had little feeling for art, and a certain contempt for artists. To hardheaded, hardworking factory owners the artist was an inefficient citizen. No one need starve in their busy world, was the manufacturers' attitude. There was work enough for all.

On the other hand these same new-rich were building costly homes, and fashion dictated that in these homes there must be art. So they were in the market to buy pictures and statues, and having no art standards of their own they turned to official sources to tell them what to buy.

This is where the Salon came in. The Salon, as we have seen, was the showcase of the Academy of Fine Arts. It had an annual show of pictures, and a jury to decide which of the pictures submitted should be hung and which rejected. If the jury refused a picture by an unknown artist the chances were that that artist would remain forever unknown. What was more dangerous (for art) was that, in order to get their paintings accepted, artists had to conform to a given standard. Their pictures had to be smooth, dignified, shining, conventional, with the result that they came to look more or less alike. The only self-assertion the artist permitted himself was to try to catch the public eye. The canvases became larger and larger, and their subjects more sensational.

This then was officially chosen art. It comprised nearly all the paintings that the public had a chance to see. And by the middle of the nineteenth century public taste had reached an all-time low.

But the true artist was a man apart. He never sacrificed his ideals to popular opinion, and by his integrity he helped bring about one of the most glowing passages in the whole story of our culture.

Chapter 9

PARIS

Paris in the late nineteenth century was the art center of the world. Not since the glory of Florence in the fifteenth century had there been such freshness, such originality, such drama among artists. Never had so many geniuses congregated in so small a space, in so few years. The names are close enough to us to ring familiar: Manet, Monet, Degas, Renoir, Van Gogh, Toulouse-Lautrec, Gauguin, Cézanne. There were many others, all working at the same time, all living in a corner of Paris. They had to endure years of rebuff and of suffering, but together they completely changed the course of art. Their period—short, vivid, alive—ranks with the best in the history of painting.

They lived in Montmartre, a little village on a steep cliff overlooking Paris during the last half of the nineteenth century.

By 1860 Montmartre had become a part of the city of Paris. But it still had its windmills, its creamy-white houses that leaned crazily, little iron balconies, old stables. Around the narrow streets rambled cows and goats and chickens, and in the small cobbled square (now Place du Tertre) old men played dominoes.

It was quaint and picturesque and cheap. It was also lively. Cafes had begun to pop up, followed by night clubs and dance halls. It was a place to work by day and play by night, a natural rendezvous for poor musicians and writers and artists. By 1860 the little village had become the center of bohemian life—of what we like to call "la vie de Bohème."

But bohemian life was not always so carefree as stories and operas would have us think, nor were all artists poor and hungry. What united these artists in Montmartre was a desire to be free to paint as they pleased. They were often rivals, often at war with one another's ideas. They belonged to no "school." But one and all were fighting against the rules which had been binding artists tighter and tighter for the past hundred years. Together they were ready to defy the Academy, the Salon, and the general public.

Paris was a city of wealth. The Empire had been restored in 1852 with Napoleon III and the Empress Eugénie at the helm, surrounded by a commonplace court. Unlike the princes of the Renaissance, these rulers had little cultivation in the arts, and their taste, like that of the people, was formed by the board of judges of the official Salon.

The artists of Montmartre rebelled against this complacency. They chose to be isolated, far from the elegance of Salon and court. They asserted their independence by wearing workmen's clothes—corduroy trousers, smocks and berets—in contrast to the flowing ties, broad-brimmed hats, and tight-fitting coats of the Academicians. They let their beards and their hair grow long. They gathered in garrets and cafes to discuss their problems. They painted in a new way, and they painted their way to fame.

The Café Guerbois was the first meeting place of these Montmartre artists, soon followed by the Café de la Nouvelle-Athénée. The man about whom they rallied was Edouard Manet.

Edouard Manet

1832–1883

Surprisingly enough Manet was to all outward appearances a conservative, and unlike the bohemian artists around him, far from unconventional in his way of living. He was a charming attractive Parisian, well-to-do, and something of a dandy. He could be seen about town wearing yellow gloves, tight trousers, a flower in his buttonhole, a fine cigar in his hand. His father was Chief of Staff in the Paris Ministry of Justice, and tried to make a lawyer out of young Edouard. But the boy had an unquenchable urge toward art, and law did not "take."

His parents next tried the navy. They got him a berth as pilot's apprentice at the age of sixteen, on a ship carrying Dutch cheeses to Brazil. But the only job that Edouard did outstandingly

MANET. Young Man in the Costume of a Majo. Metropolitan Museum of Art, New York, H. O. Havemeyer Collection, 1929.

142

MANET. Woman with Parrot. Metropolitan Museum of Art, New York, Gift of Erwin Davis.

well on the trip was painting the cheeses as they became discolored by the salt water.

When he returned the family gave in, and for the rest of his life Manet was a painter.

He was never deliberately "different." Far from disdaining public praise, nothing would have pleased Manet more than to have his paintings exhibited at the Salon year after year. But he was an artist with a conscience. He insisted on painting in his own way, and the Salon rewarded his integrity with scorn.

He did not plan to be unconventional. As a student he copied the old masters. He visited Spain and discovered Velásquez for the modern world. His early work shows the Spanish influence, and his later work the influence of Frans Hals. He did not disapprove of the past. Yet from almost every angle his approach to painting was entirely new.

Before Manet, from the early Italians on, the figures in pictures were rounded, as in low-relief sculpture. Manet painted his figures flat. He used no shadows, no shading. He scorned the shining finish that had become so popular in the Salon, and worked

143

MANET. Mlle. Victorine in the Costume of an Espada. Metropolitan Museum of Art, New York, H. O. Havemeyer Collection, 1929.

long and hard to make his own work look "unfinished," "improvised." This was anarchy. He painted only what the eye saw, and what the eye saw in one *moment of time*. His colors were bright, pure, jewel-like. No painting like this had ever before been seen.

No wonder the Salon would have none of him. Beside Manet's paintings the Salon choices looked dark and tired and all alike. To stand in front of a Manet was to catch a dazzling glimpse of a world never seen before on canvas.

"Light is the most important person in any picture!" he cried.

"What nonsense!" retorted officialdom.

In the nineteenth century artists with new ideas were suppressed. In Florence they would have been encouraged. In 1863 the Salon judges rejected 4000 paintings. This raised such a cry of protest from artists and students all over Paris that the Emperor (whose own pictures had been chosen entirely by the Salon judges) thought it might be a diplomatic move to establish a second Salon where the "rejects" could be hung, which he did. It was opened next door to the official Salon and was called the Salon des Refusés, Salon of the Rejected.

The public, encouraged by the Salon dignitaries, dropped in for a good laugh. They went to make fun, but the experience had far-reaching repercussions. The Salon continued to exhibit yearly in its same old arbitrary way. But in the rejects the people had had a glimpse of something startingly new, and in the not too distant future, public taste itself underwent a revolution.

Three of Manet's paintings hung among the rejected. "A place in the Louvre is reserved for Manet," said Zola in his newspaper account of the rejects, and lost his job for saying it. Of the three pictures in that show, two are now in the Metropolitan Museum of Art, and one is in the Louvre.

Manet's favorite model, whom he painted in these three and many other pictures, was Victorine Meurend, somewhat scornfully called the "femme fatale of 1865." Her small sharp face with its beady black eyes is nearly as well known to the present generation of gallery visitors as that of Mona Lisa. Nearly thirty years after Manet painted her, a little old woman, down and out, and in need of any kind of work, turned up in the studio of a Montmartre painter who was well known for his generosity. The old woman was Victorine, and the painter, Toulouse-Lautrec.

The Manet home became a center for artists of all kinds. His wife was a musician, so composers gathered there as well as writers and painters. Debussy was a close friend, as was Mallarmé the poet, Zola the novelist, Monet, Degas, Renoir—all of whom were revolutionary painters.

Yet for twenty years, in spite of the radical atmosphere surrounding him, Manet continued to try for the real Salon, and always failed. Once he offered to do a painting for the Paris

MANET. The Picnic. The Louvre, Paris.

MANET. Le Bon Bock. Collection of Mrs.
Carroll S. Tyson, Chestnut Hill,
Philadelphia.

Hotel de Ville (town hall) but never even got an answer from
the officials. He became sad and discouraged. In 1881 a friend con-
trived to get him the Légion d'honneur, which pleased him
mightily. But it came too late. He was already a sick man and
two years later he died.

Manet opened the door to a new civilization of art. Through it
other artists followed, each proceeding in his own direction.
Manet's everlasting importance lies not only in the beautiful
pictures he painted, but in that inner strength that made him—
against all his natural inclinations—break with the past and create
the future.

Claude Monet

1840–1926

Claude Monet, son of a small grocer in Le Havre, was one of the
true Montmartre bohemians. He was very poor. Manet helped pay
for his paints, and Renoir brought him bread. Year after year his
pictures were rejected by the Salon, and his young wife died of
malnutrition. But Monet's artistic spirit never flagged. Edouard
Manet's new vision of light consumed Monet. He even admitted
that he had studied the color effects on his wife's skin in the light
of dawn, as she lay there dead.

During the Franco-Prussian War (1870–1871), when Paris
was besieged by the Germans, Monet escaped to England. It is

146

MONET. Rouen Cathedral. Chester Dale
Collection, National Gallery of Art,
Washington, D.C.

MONET. Gare St. Lazare. The Louvre, Paris.

hard to blame him. While Bismarck and the German generals had large dinners the Parisians ate their dogs and cats; cabs had long since disappeared from the city streets because the horses that drew them had all been eaten; and before the siege was lifted the population was reduced to a diet of rats.

In London Monet came upon Turner's paintings in all their magical light. Turner and Monet had much in common. They saw the world with a fresh eye, and both were conscious of the modernity of that world. To show the airy light in steam Turner had painted an English railroad station, and for the same reason Monet painted *Gare St. Lazare,* the railroad station in Paris. Before them no one would have dreamed of putting anything so unromantic into a picture.

Back in Paris in 1874, Monet hit upon what turned out to be an epoch-making idea. He persuaded his painter friends in Montmartre to have a Group exhibition of their own. It took months of arguing and arranging, but finally thirty painters assembled 165 of their own pictures and hung them in the studio of a photographer named Nadar. It was one of the outstanding events in the history of art.

"Five or six lunatics, among them a woman, have joined together . . ." wrote one critic.

The lunatics included Renoir, Degas, Sisley, Pissarro, Berthe Morisot, and Cézanne.

148

Crowds of sightseers piled into the exhibition. They went partly to satisfy their curiosity but chiefly to ridicule. The title of one picture by Monet contained the word *"impression,"* and the public seized upon it.

"Impressionists!" they cried derisively. And the name stuck.

Impressionism has now come to stand for that new movement in art that came about in the late nineteenth century. It has come to stand for certain painters, not the same in all lists, and for certain methods, often quite different, about which people have never stopped quarreling.

It all started with three young painters, Monet, Renoir, and Pissarro, who used to sit on the bank of the Seine River painting landscapes. The reflection of light on the water challenged them—the continuous movement, sparkle, life—with no shadows and no dark tones. How to paint it!

Their frenzied impulse to catch this ever-changing light gradually developed into a new painting method. Outdoors, with the light constantly different, there was no time to mix colors. Before this, artists had painted with a certain amount of leisure. Now they had to finish a painting at a sitting. They painted in rapid strokes, covered their canvases with hundreds of small dabs of paint, and put colors beside each other which, from a distance, blended into the colors they wanted to produce. They mixed color in the eye of the spectator, as it were, instead of on the palette. For instance, if they wished to produce green they put yellow and blue beside each other which created a brighter effect than if they mixed them together first. They went by no rule. They just sensed the right combination. But by this apparently haphazard dividing of colors—"broken colors" it is called—they built the foundation of modern art.

Monet was the first painter to be called an Impressionist. He abandoned his studio altogether and painted outdoors. He painted the same things over and over again at different times of day to get the different effects of light—water lilies, haystacks, Rouen Cathedral. He once exhibited fifteen pictures of the same haystack in one gallery. He painted Rouen Cathedral forty times.

The effect was dazzling. But in the flickering of light reality was almost lost. Sometimes Rouen Cathedral seems to sway (see page 147).

The Impressionists had eight exhibitions from 1874 to 1886. During that period, though new names appeared from time to time, the purpose for which the painters originally organized was accomplished: the public became aware of them, and their pictures eventually began to sell.

By 1890 Monet's fortunes took a turn. He married a wealthy widow, became a close friend of the successful sculptor Rodin, and above all, with his shimmering canvases he caught the public fancy. His pictures soared in price. From ten francs one went to 100,000 francs. But as soon as fortune smiled upon him, the other artists turned away. Still newer ideas were coming up.

Monet's career as an artist lasted sixty years. Toward the end his eyesight was failing, yet he sometimes painted as many as ten pictures a day. He died at the good old age of eighty-six.

SISLEY. Bridge at Villeneuve. John G.
Johnson Collection, Philadelphia.

Sisley and Pissarro were two of the painters whose work followed closely that of Monet. ALFRED SISLEY (1837–1899) was born of well-to-do English parents in Paris, who lost everything in the war of 1870. All his adult life Sisley was poor. He had a wife and several children and could not sell a painting. Manet introduced him to a restaurant owner who sometimes accepted Sisley's pictures in payment for food—because he himself was something of a painter. During his whole life Sisley never got more than twenty-five or thirty francs for a picture, and his death was probably brought on by worry and poverty. He died of cancer in 1899, and the very next year, in 1900, the Impressionists suddenly became fashionable, and his paintings brought large prices. The best known are his landscapes.

CAMILLE PISSARRO (1830–1903) was born on the island of St. Thomas in the Caribbean, of a Creole mother and a French Jewish father. His father, an ironmonger, wanted his son brought up in Paris, but he warned the master of the school to which he

PISSARRO. Afternoon at the Boulevard
des Italiens. Private Collection.

sent him that the boy had crazy notions about wanting to paint.

The crazy notions eventually brought him friends—Monet and Renoir and Sisley.

He went with Monet to London during the Franco-Prussian War, and while he was gone the Germans occupied his house outside Paris and used it as a butcher shop. They destroyed all his 1500 canvases, as well as some of Monet's that were stored there. He was one of the original group that exhibited in the photographer's salon in 1874, and the only one to exhibit in all eight of the group shows. He was a friend of Cézanne, who antagonized everybody else, and had he not encouraged Gauguin, that strange man might never have become a painter. Pissarro was indeed the friendliest and the kindest of all the Montmartre painters, and when he died at seventy-three, the world of artists mourned.

Pissarro the painter went through many phases, but he will be longest remembered as a true early Impressionist. His Paris scenes are among his most famous pictures.

Edgar Degas

1834–1917

Like Manet, Edgar Degas was a man of means. He was the son of a banker, born in the South of France.

Unlike Monet (and Sisley and Pissarro) he was not absorbed exclusively, as a painter, in problems of light and air. He refused to paint outdoors. When exposed to Monet's paintings he would turn up the collar of his coat, and say, "I hate drafts."

As a young man Degas studied under a pupil of Ingres. "Lines, lines, lines," was the Ingres dictum, and Degas drew lines until he became one of the finest draughtsmen of the century. Since he was traditional to this extent, his pictures were accepted regularly for the Salon.

DEGAS. At the Milliner's. Metropolitan Museum of Art, New York, H. O. Havemeyer Collection.

151

Yet he was one of the Impressionists. He lived among them in Montmartre, though he wore English tweeds instead of corduroy. He changed his aristocratic name from De Gas to Degas. He helped organize the Group exhibits, and had his own paintings hanging in them for six years, though he had far more to lose than gain by joining the so-called "lunatics." He was indifferent to the Salon. Whether or not they took his paintings made no difference. And though Manet was his friend, Degas despised him when he accepted the official Légion d'honneur.

Degas's strong bond with the Impressionists was their common revolt against convention and the established order. This was a new world, and the Impressionists showed themselves a part of it. Like both Manet and Monet, Degas was through with romance and make-believe. He wanted no poses, no prettiness. The world of his day was the world of his art. He painted Paris life in cafes, theater, opera, on the race track. He particularly liked to paint the ballet from the wings where he could catch the dancers off guard, or from a box where he could see them at an odd angle. In his studio he never had his models pose, but asked them to walk about while he painted. One can feel the bones and muscle in his ballet girls, yet Degas got his effect only by suggestion, never by actual detail. Even more than Manet he tried for the casual gesture, the fleeting moment, the "camera's click," which makes his figures so alive. The more spontaneous they look the harder they were to paint.

When the Franco-Prussian War broke out, Degas, unlike Monet, enlisted. He was in the artillery. After the war he took the long trip to New Orleans in America, where his mother had been born and where the family was fast losing money in cotton speculation. He tried to straighten out the financial situation and at the same time painted some pictures there.

But most of his life was spent in a shabby old house in Montmartre where he lived alone, a rather disagreeable, unsociable man whom the other artists rarely visited because of his sharp tongue. When asked why he never married he said, "I would be afraid, upon finishing a painting, to hear my wife say to me, 'What you have done there is very pretty!'"

DEGAS. Before the Ballet. Widener Collection, National Gallery of Art, Washington, D.C.

DEGAS. Study for a Portrait of Edouard Manet, lead pencil. Metropolitan Museum of Art, New York, Rogers Fund, 1918.

His only love was pictures. He had a fine collection of Ingres and Delacroix and, of the later artists, Cézanne and Gauguin. He hated to part with his own pictures and when he did go so far as to sell them he sometimes borrowed them back and "forgot" to return them. (One man, knowing this idiosyncrasy, chained his Degas paintings to the wall, padlocked them, and deliberately lost the keys.)

Degas was furious when a certain painting of his was resold for 19,000 pounds, knowing how little the original buyer paid. "I'm like a horse who has won the race without having his ration of oats increased!"

153

DEGAS. The Cotton Market, New Orleans.
Pau Museum, Pau.

After the last Impressionist exhibit in 1886, Degas never offered another picture for exhibition. But he painted more diligently than ever. His eyesight was bad and he lived in constant fear of blindness, which made him more feverish and intense about his work, more difficult to get along with. It also made him rely more on pastel than oil, and he is one of the few artists whose best work is done in that medium. Pastel is a kind of crayon in which dried paste is ground up with chalk and mixed with a gum liquid. Usually a pastel drawing cannot be retouched. But Degas used a special fixative on his pastels which allowed him to work them over, and thus to give them the depth and solidity of oil. This fixative was made by a secret process never disclosed.

Eventually Degas became totally blind.

For all his irascibility Degas was most helpful to young painters, among them Mary Cassatt, an American, who owed her success to his appreciation of her artistic talent.

In the case of the two famous women Impressionists, Berthe Morisot and Mary Cassatt, it is interesting to note that their parents, unlike the parents of male artists, were more than willing to have their daughters take up the profession of painting.

154

DEGAS. Portrait of Mary Cassatt.
Collection of André Meyer.

MORISOT. Girl with a Basket. Collection
of Mrs. Carroll S. Tyson, Chestnut Hill,
Philadelphia

BERTHE MORISOT (1841–1895) was the daughter of a man who
himself had studied art and was naturally sympathetic with his
daughter's artistic leanings. She became a pupil of Corot, and
under his tutelage had many pictures hung in the Salon. But
everything changed on the day she chanced to meet Edouard Manet
in the Louvre, where she was copying pictures. It was a case of
mutual artistic admiration. Soon she became his pupil, through
him was introduced to the exciting Impressionist circle, and
actually became one of the original Group exhibit in 1874. She was
one of the "lunatics," as well as one of France's greatest women
painters. She married Manet's brother Eugène.

Her paintings are delightful in the bright fresh Manet style,
which she made her own.

MARY CASSATT (1845–1926) was born in Allegheny City, Pennsylvania. As a girl she studied cast drawing at the Philadelphia Academy of Art, but soon realized that this was not what she wanted. So at the age of twenty she went to Europe to visit the galleries and study the old masters. She went to Madrid and to Antwerp, where the lush paintings of Rubens swept her off her prim Pennsylvania feet. Eventually she found her place in Paris, settled there, and was joined by her family.

Like Berthe Morisot she, too, had many paintings accepted by the Salon, and like Berthe she had the inspiration that comes only from a truly great artist. Degas became a close friend, and advised and exhorted her. She was the only American artist whose paintings were hung with the Impressionists.

Like her master she also went blind, which is probably the most tragic fate that can befall a painter. She lived out her long life in France, alone in the last years.

Her best-known pictures are those on the mother-and-child theme.

157

CASSATT. Mother and Child. Philadelphia
Museum of Art, Philadelphia.

The artist upon whom Degas had perhaps the most far-reaching effect was Toulouse-Lautrec.

HENRI DE TOULOUSE-LAUTREC (1864–1901) stands alone. He was not an Impressionist. He defies classification. But he idolized Degas.

Like Degas he leaned toward drawing rather than toward color. Light meant little to him. Only human beings counted. He painted indoors, by gaslight rather than sunshine. Like Degas he chose odd angles from which to view his model. Even more ruthlessly than Degas he reproduced the bizarre life of Montmartre.

Toulouse-Lautrec, because we have heard so much about him (not always true) from the many books and films on his life, personifies the dark romance of bohemian life. He was a descendant of two of the oldest families in France, was born in the town of Albi in the South of France, and lived his childhood on the big hunting estates of his family. His father, Count Alphonse, was

TOULOUSE-LAUTREC. Yvette Guilbert. Albi Museum, Albi.

158

TOULOUSE-LAUTREC. Au Moulin Rouge, (*detail below*). The Art Institute of Chicago, Chicago, Helen Birch Bartlett Memorial Collection.

a strange figure whose eccentricities might have been reflected in his son's wild ways. He was completely unconventional. One day he would wear Scotch kilts, another day a suit of armor as the mood dictated. He was so absent-minded that he once went off leaving his young wife waiting on a railroad station platform with no money; he frequently forgot her in the mad Paris whirl. But he kept a chest well filled with money in the Lautrec household, into which both he and the Countess dipped their hands as they wished.

Henri was a fragile child. When he was fourteen he slipped on a polished floor and broke his leg. It never healed. The next year, while walking with his mother, he fell again and broke the other leg. Neither leg grew, and the unfortunate youth, with everything else in the world to make him happy, grew up into a misshapen dwarf with normal body and short legs. He was only four feet six inches tall.

When he was twenty-three, in 1887, this strange figure went up to Paris and settled in Montmartre. He was crippled, his skin was dark and oily, he had a black wiry beard, and wore thick eyeglasses on a black ribbon. In no other place than Montmartre would his ugly appearance have been so easily accepted, or his natural genius so appreciated. In *Au Moulin Rouge* the artist is the short man walking beside the tall one in the rear.

Lautrec was proud and sensitive and highly intelligent. He was also already an accomplished painter, and his studio soon became the heart of bohemia. Artists, writers, wits, dancers, singers danced

and sang and argued late into the night. Drinks flowed. Food was more plentiful here than anywhere else in Montmartre. But while the parties were at their height the host might often be seen sitting at his easel hard at work.

His life was tied up with his art. He flaunted respectability, and lived with the disreputable figures whom he chose to paint—perhaps because he found in them a reflection of his own frustration. He understood these people.

But he lived too hard, and drank too hard. When the Prince of Wales visited his show in one of the Paris galleries Lautrec was asleep on the sofa, probably drunk. In 1890 he had a nervous breakdown and was sent to a sanitarium. To prove that his mind was in good working order he painted fifty pictures in the three months he was there, then wrote to his father, "Dear Papa, Here is an opportunity for you to act like a good man. I am imprisoned and everything that is imprisoned dies . . ." But his father never answered the letter. His mother, however, hovered not too faraway, keeping a sad shocked eye on her Henri. When he died, three years later, at the age of thirty-seven, she went over the work in his studio and gave many of his canvases to the town of Albi, where he was born.

Lautrec was the first great painter to do posters. It was a form well suited to his particular genius—art in a few strokes, simplified, exaggerated, seemingly improvised. He did posters for cafes and theaters and bookstores. In both his posters and his paintings there is an unmistakable light touch, perfection in drawing, and bold originality in color—a combination that has never been duplicated.

TOULOUSE-LAUTREC. The Clown Mlle. Cha-U-Kao. The Art Institute of Chicago, Chicago, Charles F. Glore Collection.

160

RENCIR. Mme. Charpentier and Her Children. Metropolitan Museum of Art, New York, Wolfe Fund, 1907.

Auguste Renoir

1841–1919

Auguste Renoir loved life. He was a joyous painter who sang as he worked.

Born in Limoges, he was the son of a poor tailor, and all his life, as with Turner, his speech remained that of the working class. Servants in other peoples' houses treated him like one of themselves, which was fine with Renoir, who was, above all, simple, wholesome, and elemental. He despised pretentious people as much as he disliked pretentious speech.

When he came to Paris and found his way to Montmartre he was a handsome young man with pink-and-white complexion, merry eyes, tousled black hair, and a battered old hat on the back of his head. All the waitresses, models, laundresses, and seamstresses on the Butte adored him. He danced and sang, and went with them on picnics and boating parties. He treated all alike.

Renoir wanted to be a painter, and at twenty-one entered an art studio where he met two other struggling young artists, Monet and Sisley. To pay his expenses Renoir took a job painting pottery. He had learned the trade in his home town of Limoges,

161

noted for the finest china in France, and now—for five cents a dozen—he painted on cups and saucers the pretty ladies he would one day paint on canvas. He started at two sous a dessert plate, and three sous for Marie Antoinette in profile. He also painted figures on fans and window shades. He got himself an attic in Montmartre and spent his noon hours at the Louvre.

Renoir became a close friend of the Montmartre artists and was one of the famous original Group that exhibited in 1874. He exhibited with them again in 1876 and 1878. Then he quit.

Unlike Manet, Renoir was willing to compromise. When he received a commission to paint the portrait of a lady of importance with her children, he abandoned Impressionism and all radical ideas, and painted her as she wanted to be painted. This was a conventional picture that won instant public approval and delighted the lady. She was Mme. Charpentier, wife of a successful publisher, who had a literary salon of her own, and now became Renoir's patroness (see page 161).

Renoir's reputation was made. But instead of staying on in Paris, where orders began to pick up, he took himself off to study the

RENOIR. Le Moulin de la Galette. The Louvre, Paris.

RENOIR. Le Moulin de la Galette (detail). The Louvre, Paris.

great masters. He was dissatisfied with himself; and with the money he received for the Charpentier portrait he visited Algiers, got married, and made an art pilgrimage to Italy. He was particularly interested in Raphael and basked in the work of the Venetians.

During the Italian trip he visited Wagner in Palermo and painted his portrait. The composer sat for twenty minutes, then said he was tired, and left. It was on that very day, January 15, 1883, that he finished his opera *Parsifal.*

But neither popularity nor the old masters left a perceptible mark on Renoir in the long run. Through the years of painting that followed, he returned to his early ideals and became one of the outstanding Impressionists. Carefree happiness pervades his paintings. His colors sing with yellow, pinks, greens, blue—the so-called "rainbow palette." His ladies look like peaches, his peaches like ladies.

He was Degas's opposite. Where Degas tried to catch just one moment of existence—the corner of a stage, a single gesture— Renoir painted beauty that was everlasting. Degas's women were plain almost to the point of ugliness. Renoir could not paint a woman without making her lovely. Toulouse-Lautrec, going a step further than Degas, had already painted cabaret dancers. Renoir painted serene calm women. To him woman was a symbol of life, as she had been to the Greeks, to the Venetians, and to a long line of French painters, of whom Renoir was in the true tradition.

163

RENOIR. At the Piano (*left*). The Art
Institute of Chicago, Chicago, Mr. and
Mrs. Martin A. Ryerson Collection.

RENOIR. In the Meadow (*right*). Metropolitan Museum of Art, New York, Bequest of Samuel A. Lewisohn, 1951.

Though Renoir specialized in lovely red heads, he did through
the years paint two particular girls, one of whom was a brunette,
the other a blonde. We see them first seated at the piano; later in
the meadow; sometimes nude as bathers; finally as young ladies
all dressed up in their best, sitting on stiff little chairs.

During the last fifteen years of his life Renoir suffered constant
agonizing pain from arthritis. He could not walk but had to be
lifted out of a wheel chair and carried to his studio. He grew gray
and emaciated, his body became more and more petrified, his fin-
gers curled inward. Yet he continued to paint. His skin was so
tender that he could not bear the rubbing of a brush against it, and
his son inserted a piece of cloth into the hollow of his hand before
putting the brush into it. Only then could he paint. But he was
joyous still, happy to be alive, happy to capture the color of the
world around him, and during that period of incredible suffering
he produced some of his greatest work.

Georges Seurat

1859–1891

Georges Seurat was a shy young man. He never married. He kept
to himself, apart from other painters, scarcely sold a painting in his
life, and died at thirty-one. Yet he left one of the most famous
paintings in the world.

Although Seurat was in love with his model, Madeleine Knob-
lock, and she bore him a son, not one of his friends knew of the

relationship until after his death. But science, which has unearthed many a secret, has also disclosed Seurat's. His only portrait was one of Madeleine, which he called *La Poudreuse*. In the picture frame on the wall behind the sitter, where there is now a vase of flowers, he had originally painted his own portrait. This was disclosed not long ago by X-ray. Including himself in the picture of Madeleine had no doubt been his tribute to their affection and intimacy. Painting over it was one more mark of his desire for privacy and withdrawal.

Seurat was born in Paris, the son of a bailiff, who was an odd-looking character with a hook in place of the hand he had lost in an accident. The family dwelling was an apartment in Paris, but Papa Seurat visited it only once a week, spending the rest of his leisure time in a villa outside the city, where he had a private chapel. The whole family was united, however, during the bombardment of Paris, 1870–1871, and lived together in Fontainebleau.

After the war the young Seurat attended the Beaux Arts, the academic art school of Paris, where he studied with a pupil of Ingres, learning to draw "lines and lines," and working almost entirely in black and white. He made no great mark in the school and ranked only forty-seventh when he left at the end of two years.

Apparently it was after that that he discovered Impressionism, because from 1882 until he died nine years later, he devoted himself wholly to the mastery of color. At school he had learned to draw lines. Now he began to make drawings which had no lines, only varying tones of color.

Like the Impressionists, he painted the world around him— Parisian figures, landscape, sunshine, light effects. But unlike the

SEURAT. La Poudreuse. Courtauld Institute, London.

165

others he was not interested in catching that fleeting moment. He wanted permanence and exactness. Out of Monet's haphazard lack of technique, Seurat developed a science. He, too, painted in dabs of color, but in thousands upon thousands of dabs, tiny circular dots of color, like confetti, applied with painstaking precision and built up into solid forms. This way of painting is called Pointillism. There is no haziness here, no swaying—but the beautiful eternal stillness of a Piero della Francesca.

Pointillism did not have many immediate followers. But Seurat's scientific approach foreshadowed the art of today. Through the work of Cézanne it led ultimately to the abstract art of Picasso.

No painter of the Renaissance worked harder than Seurat—all day long and far into the night. For two years he concentrated with infinite patience on a single picture. He made preliminary drawings, painted sketches, and worked out effects of light and shadow. It was a landscape with figures which he called *A Sunday Afternoon on the Grande Jatte*. It was hung in the last Impressionist exhibit, in 1886, and the public hooted.

The *Grande Jatte* is a large painting of Parisians enjoying themselves beside a river in the sun, a subject that should appeal to anyone. The design is perfection. The curves—of parasol, bustles, heads—are in the most exquisite taste. The molded figures, the straight trees, are almost classical. The composition is as elegant and calm and eternal as a Raphael. But the public would have none of it, and even Seurat's fellow artists frowned. Perhaps his canvas was too large, and his technique too strange. Who can say?

Worn out with work Seurat died at thirty-one of a quinsy sore throat. Only ten days before his death he visited the Group show where his picture *Le Cirque* (see page 169) was hung. He watched Puvis de Chavannes, at that time probably the most popular and the most famous painter in Paris. Chavannes passed by the Seurat picture without even glancing at it.

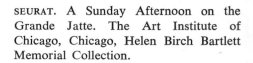
SEURAT. A Sunday Afternoon on the Grande Jatte. The Art Institute of Chicago, Chicago, Helen Birch Bartlett Memorial Collection.

SEURAT. A Sunday afternoon on the
Grande Jatte (detail). The Art Institute
of Chicago, Chicago, Helen Birch
Bartlett Memorial Collection.

SEURAT. La Parade (*detail below*). Metropolitan Museum of Art, New York, Bequest of Stephen C. Clark, 1960.

SEURAT. Le Cirque. The Louvre, Paris.

At the time of Seurat's death all of his paintings still hung in his studio, unsold—seven large pictures and forty small ones. Even as late as 1900, when Impressionism was definitely "in," the *Grande Jatte* brought only 900 francs. An American collector, John Quinn, gave *Le Cirque* to the French Government but the government accepted it without enthusiasm. Of his six large pictures it is the only one now in Paris.

Today *Grande Jatte* hangs in all its glory in the Art Institute of Chicago. The Institute was offered a million dollars for its return to France not long ago, and refused the offer.

Vincent Van Gogh

1853–1890

Poor Vincent Van Gogh! We know almost as much about his misfortunes as we know about Lautrec's misdemeanors. Many books have been written about him, a film done on his pictures, and his letters to his brother Theo leave scarcely a thought unturned.

He was a scrawny little man with a thin red beard and bright blue eyes. A Dutchman, he was the son of a minister and was himself deeply religious. Though he studied for the ministry he could not get through the seminary, so went instead to live as an unordained minister among the Belgian coal miners.

His deepest desire was to help the poor, but he never knew quite how to go about it. He dressed untidily, believing that the less he looked like a well-to-do person the closer he would be to

169

VAN GOGH. The Starry Night. Permanent
Collection, The Museum of Modern Art,
New York, Acquired through the Lillie
P. Bliss Bequest.

the poor. People laughed at him. When he was with the miners he
lived as they lived. He slept on a board with a straw mattress.
The miners shrugged their shoulders. Why shouldn't a man dress
well and be comfortable if he could afford it? They were also a little afraid. His odd personality made them uneasy.

When he tried to sell pictures in a gallery he was equally a
failure. He had an uncle in the art business who tried him out as a
salesman in The Hague, in London, and in Paris, but nowhere
could poor Vincent sell a picture.

All his life he was frustrated. He wanted friends but could not
keep them because he was so high-strung and nervous. His three
love affairs ended in disaster.

Vincent's younger brother Theo was manager of an art dealer's
shop on Boulevard Montmartre, which dealt in Impressionist paintings. Through him Vincent came to know several of the Montmartre artists, Toulouse-Lautrec, Gauguin, Seurat. He had tried
painting before, but this personal introduction in the heart of
Montmartre stirred him so deeply that painting soon took preced-
ence over all other interests.

He came into his own as an artist when he went to live in Arles
in the South of France. Theo, who had supported him in Paris,
now financed his trip south. In Arles Vincent opened like a flower.

"The sun pours down bright yellow rays on the shrubs and the earth in an absolute shower of gold!" he wrote Theo. He painted his little house yellow, decorated it with large sunflowers and called it "The House of Friends." As with the Belgian miners, the villagers of Arles looked at him askance and treated him like the village idiot.

He painted in a frenzy of excitement. Unlike the Impressionists he did not try to catch the changing light and color, or to paint objects as they really existed. He painted only to fit his mood. His flowers were flamelike, his trees twisted, grass swayed, roadways writhed. His brushstrokes were short and thick and violent, like his own fervor.

Painting of this kind is called Expressionism. Impressionism conveys what the artist sees with his eye, Expressionism what he sees with his mind. The springboard for Impressionism is thus visual, Expressionism psychological. Expressionism is a term used in reference to modern art only. But actually it was to be found in El Greco who distorted form and color to suit himself. But where he did it for its striking effect, Van Gogh did it only from an inner urge. He changed nature, exaggerated it, distorted it—only to fit his own violent moods.

Van Gogh was a lonely man. In Paris he had met the painter Paul Gauguin and greatly admired him. Now he invited Gauguin to come down to Arles to live with him and paint. But like all his other attempts at love and friendship, this relationship ended in failure. Gauguin was at that time a hearty, handsome, outgoing

VAN GOGH. L'Arlésienne. Metropolitan Museum of Art, New York, Samuel A. Lewisohn Collection.

171

VAN GOGH. Sunflowers. Collection of
Mrs. Carroll S. Tyson, Chestnut Hill,
Philadelphia.

VAN GOGH. The Stairway at Auvers.
Collection, City Art Museum of St. Louis,
St. Louis.

VAN GOGH. The Olive Orchard. Chester Dale Collection, National Gallery of Art, Washington, D.C.

man. His painting was at the opposite pole from Van Gogh's, and the two quarreled incessantly. Once the quarrel got so violent that Vincent chased Gauguin with a razor. Then, in a fit of remorse, he rushed to his own room and cut off one of his ears.

He could not keep a friend, he could not paint a picture that would sell. His urgent desire now was somehow to repay his brother Theo for his support through all these years, and he worked feverishly toward that end. Finally he broke down. He had a series of attacks of what may have been epilepsy, and ended up in a mental hospital in Arles, where he stayed on and off for the next two and a half years. It was at this time that he painted the magnificent pictures by which the world knows him best.

In July 1890 Van Gogh ended his own life, at thirty-seven. He had returned to Paris and Theo had put him into the care of a doctor who was the friend and adviser of many artists. Six months after Vincent's death, Theo died, insane.

It is said that in all his life Vincent Van Gogh sold only one picture. Now his paintings are probably the most popular and well-known of all modern art. They are reproduced on calendars, in schools, in nurseries, which is just as he would have wished it. "I should like to paint in such a way that anyone with two eyes could understand." And he succeeded.

173

GAUGUIN. Self-portrait. Chester Dale Collection, National Gallery of Art, Washington, D.C.

Paul Gauguin

1848–1903

Paul Gauguin was a "Sunday painter": on weekdays he was a successful Parisian stockbroker, and on Sundays he painted for recreation. He was an amateur who never thought seriously of art until he was nearly middle-aged. His financial investments were successful, he had a wife and children, and lived a pleasant family life. He liked pictures and was discerning enough to see the artistic worth of the original Impressionist Group and to buy some of their paintings.

About the time of this first show he met Pissarro—an event which turned out to be earth-shaking in its results. Pissarro, who lived only for art, planted a germ in the conventional stockbroker that completely overthrew his life. He introduced him to Manet and Degas. He took him to the Café Nouvelle-Athénée to listen to the discussions, and fired him with artistic ambition. Gauguin now began to paint seriously, and when the Montmartre artists continued to regard him as an amateur, he threw up his job and income and gave himself up entirely to painting.

Not unnaturally, his wife objected. So he took her back to Copenhagen, her birthplace, and left her there with four of their five children, he himself taking the oldest boy, Clovis. He sold his collection of Impressionist paintings to his Danish brother-in-law, and gave the proceeds to his wife.

With a child to take care of Gauguin had to have money: he tried to sell sun blinds, posted handbills, and finally went to Panama to work on the canal which was then being built, sending Clovis back to his mother. From Panama he visited the island of Martinique. There he got his first taste of the truly simple life, which soon became an obsession.

He went to Brittany to paint the peasants in the fields, and to Arles with Van Gogh, as we have seen. But the climax came when he set sail in 1891 for Tahiti, in the South Seas.

Gauguin took bohemianism to the South Seas with him. He went native in his own way, lived in a little wooden hut far in the interior, made friends with the natives, got himself a young Tahitian wife, and painted happily all day long, naked in the sun.

Gauguin and Tahiti are inextricably bound together. He painted exotic jungle foliage, and large brown monumental women with thick legs and big feet. These were not the women he saw in Tahiti, who were quite slender, but creatures of his mind—not real women but symbols of earthiness.

His way of painting was all his own. His large, simple figures were outlined in black. There was no attempt to model them and

IA ORANA MARIA

GAUGUIN. Ia Orana Maria. Metropolitan Museum of Art, New York, Samuel A. Lewisohn Collection.

175

GAUGUIN. Tahitian Landscape. The Minneapolis Institute of Arts, Minneapolis.

no attempt to suggest space around them. All the efforts of artists for the past three hundred years he threw to the winds.

Unlike the Impressionists he did not use dabs of color but large flat areas of strong solid color. The actual colors in nature made no difference: a field could be purple, a tree could be red, a face green if these colors added one whit to the decorativeness of his picture. He was against conventional painting as he was against conventional living. He rearranged nature to suit himself.

Only once did Gauguin return to Paris—a "heavy-eyed, hawk-nosed giant" of a man, wearing a long blue coat and putty-colored trousers, an astrakhan cap and white kid gloves. He had painted sixty or more pictures in Tahiti and had come back to sell them. But the dealers were not interested. While in France, however, he received an inheritance from an uncle who had died, and spent it all in one big bout of dissipation that lasted a year and a half. When he went back to Tahiti he was a wreck: alcoholic, ill, and with a broken foot—broken in a brawl—which would not heal.

The simple life was now desperately hard. He was so poor that he had to beg bread of the natives, and in the end had nothing to eat but mangoes. His illness made him intensely disagreeable, and he got in serious trouble with the authorities. He moved to the Marquesas Islands, and there he died—in long-drawn horrible agony.

176

As a colorist Gauguin was a forerunner of the "Fauves," of whom Matisse became the best known. This was a group of painters who got their name, "Wild Beasts," as casually as the Impressionists got theirs, at an exhibition. Gauguin's "Primitivism" left its mark on such differing artists as Henri Rousseau, the little French customs officer, Marc Chagall, the Russian, still painting, and Grant Wood, the American from Iowa.

Paul Cézanne

1839–1906

Paul Cézanne was the third and perhaps the greatest of the three lone figures who, unappreciated in their own time, sacrificed their lives to their art and left the strongest imprint on the painting of today. Van Gogh, Gauguin, and Cézanne were ridiculed throughout their lives, yet they are the link that joins the nineteenth and twentieth centuries—particularly Cézanne.

Fortunately for art Paul Cézanne was well-to-do. He did not have to die in hunger like Gauguin, or of frustration like poor Vincent Van Gogh. His father was a banker of Aix-en-Provence in the South of France, and even though he disapproved, he supported his son as an artist till he was twenty-three and upon his death left him a large estate.

CÉZANNE. Self-portrait. Phillips Collection, Washington, D.C.

177

CÉZANNE. Mme. Cézanne in the Conservatory. Metropolitan Museum of Art, New York, Bequest of Stephen C. Clark, 1960.

Zola, the novelist-journalist whose life and writings are intertwined with the Montmartre artists, also came from Aix. He was a close boyhood friend of Cézanne. In the school band Cézanne played the cornet and Zola the clarinet, and it was Zola who prevailed upon Paul's father to let Paul go with him to Paris. Once in Paris the two young men quickly converged upon Montmartre. The year was 1863 and the Salon of the Rejected was the talk of the town. They found the Café Nouvelle-Athénée, and joined the group gathered around Manet. They had "arrived."

But Cézanne was never easy in the role of a bohemian. He was a countryman at heart, shy and awkward. He had a homely face and an odd southern accent, unattractive to Parisian ears. To cover up his awkwardness he swaggered, and was by turns surly and impudent, which did not add to his popularity. The only artist he really liked, and who liked him, was the ever kind and gentle Pissarro.

Cézanne stayed in Paris for ten long years, spending the summers painting with Pissarro in the country, summers that were of inestimable value to his art. With Pissarro he learned to look on nature with a curious contemplative eye. Pissarro and Renoir, both of whom appreciated the awkward southerner's work, persuaded him to exhibit with them in two of their Group shows, the famous first show in 1874, and again in 1877. But the reception of his pictures was disastrous.

"Sublime ignoramus," "a jackass painting with his tail," "butcher," were some of the epithets hurled at him. The public disapproved of all the Impressionists, but with a difference. They considered Monet, Renoir, and Pissarro clever painters gone wrong. But Cézanne, they said, could neither paint nor draw. "If a child had drawn it on his slate his mother would have whipped him," said Whistler, the famous American artist. Even Cézanne's best friend, Zola, deserted him.

But Cézanne believed in himself. At the age of forty-seven he returned to Aix and painted there, forgotten by the world, for the rest of his life. He married a simple woman who understood nothing at all about his work, but who at least was always willing to pose for him, much as she disliked sitting silent. Their son, Paul, was a constant joy and satisfaction. Cézanne had come into his inheritance and was financially independent. On all counts he could live in peace. Instead he tortured himself to the day of his death, trying to work out his almost insurmountable problems.

These intricate problems which Cézanne created for himself are difficult even for painters to understand. He had tasted Impressionism and found it wanting. To his way of thinking the Impressionists had sacrificed order and balance in their urge to catch that fleeting moment in nature. What he wanted was to combine the *color* of Impressionism with the solidity of classical art. He did not want his pictures flat like Manet's or quivering like Monet's, but firm and enduring, "like the art of the museums," as he put it.

What Cézanne did for art to come was as revolutionary as what Giotto did for the Renaissance. Up to Cézanne's time painters had tried to present, in their own varying ways, the visible world. A man looked like a man, a cup like a cup. But Cézanne changed the visible world to serve his own ends. He wanted balance and design. If nature did not fit into his design then he changed nature. As Matisse said, "That isn't a woman, it's a painting!" In *Still Life with Ginger Jar* the edges of the table could not possibly meet un-

CÉZANNE. Still Life with Ginger Jar, Metropolitan Museum of Art, New York, Bequest of Stephen C. Clark, 1960.

CÉZANNE. Landscape with Viaduct.
Metropolitan Museum of Art, New York,
Bequest of Mrs. H. O. Havemeyer, 1929.
H. O. Havemeyer Collection.

der the cloth, the cloth itself is the consistency of cotton padding, the dish on which the fruit rests is lopsided, the fruit is oddly shaped. Yet the whole is solid and alive and fits the composition which the painter conceived.

Cézanne studied geometry and applied it to art: an apple feels round in the hand, but to the eye it is broken up into planes of differing color and tone. So he studied the planes, cubes, cones, and cylinders that go to make up the structure of objects whether they be apples, a mountain, or his wife's face.

Physical beauty is missing in most of Cézanne's work, as in most modern art. Nowadays one uses the word "expressive" instead of "beautiful." But there is a deeply satisfying simplicity and directness in all Cézanne pictures. This he achieved partly by putting his figures and his mountains and his towns in the middle of the canvas, and painting his people full face. But the surfaces of his moun-

180

tains, fields, coats, houses, apples are far from simple with their ever-changing, multitudinous colors.

He was a perfectionist, strange as that may seem to those who are seeing his pictures for the first time. He demanded the impossible of himself. If he was dissatisfied with paintings, he threw them out the window, or gave them to his little son to cut up for games, or to the farmers in the neighborhood, who stuck them away in barns or attics. He once painted a portrait of Vollard, the Paris art dealer. It required 115 sittings, and when it was finished Cézanne said, "The front of the shirt isn't bad!"

This same Vollard had come down to Aix to pick up some Cézanne canvases. With a sharp eye out for new art he had decided to try a Cézanne one-man show in Paris. He was offering 150 francs apiece for paintings, and when the farmers heard about it, though they thought he was crazy, they nonetheless rushed to their attics and sold all they had.

The Vollard show, held in 1895, was a dismal failure both financially and critically. It was called an outrage to art, a "nightmare of atrocities." But Cézanne persisted. He knew he was on the right track, hard as the going was. "There is only one painter at the present time, myself!" he said defiantly. Like Uccello he got

181

CÉZANNE. Portrait of Ambroise Vollard.
Petit Palais, Paris.

CÉZANNE. Mont-Sainte-Victoire from Les Lauves. Philadelphia Museum of Art, Philadelphia, George W. Elkins Collection.

up at all hours to work. As the peasants were starting out at dawn to work in the fields, there would be Cézanne, the estate owner, sitting in the dewy grass in front of his easel. He painted almost entirely outdoors.

Landscapes are his best and most characteristic work, and Mont-Sainte-Victoire is one of his finest subjects. He painted it many times, and his last version, *Mont-Sainte-Victoire from Les Lauves* is a splendid example of his two-fold aim: it is as monumental as a Masaccio and as fresh and glowing as an Impressionist painting. It has depth without the use of Renaissance perspective, and solid reality without conventional drawing.

One day in his sixty-eighth year, while painting in a driving rain, Cézanne got a chill, but he kept right on. When he finally started for home, carrying all his heavy painting paraphernalia, he collapsed on the road and was picked up by a laundry cart. A week later he died.

Cézanne created an era in the history of painting. His use of planes and cubes led to Cubism. His distortion of nature to fit his own scheme of design is echoed in a hundred different ways. And his simplification of form opened the way to abstract art. He is the father of today's art.

182

And the Story of Art
Goes On . . .

It has been a magnificent procession.

Giotto, emerging from the miracles and myths and sweet mysteriousness of the Middle Ages, who began a new epoch in art by reaching for reality, by attempting to paint real people who could weep and pray and pity.

Masaccio, who a hundred years after Giotto achieved Giotto's dream in monumental figures.

Piero della Francesca, who added to Masaccio's simplicity a new light, a new color, a calm new beauty.

Botticelli, whose ideal of grace was the essence of the Early Renaissance.

We have seen *Florence,* center of the glorious awakening, the eager people, the Medici leaders who nurtured great art, the era of learning and of taste.

Rome with its wealth, the gathering place for the civilized and the ambitious.

Leonardo with his commanding intellect, his comprehension of a new world of science, his unflinching pursuit of knowledge, and the wondrous spiritual beauty of the women he painted.

PICASSO. Les Demoiselles d'Avignon. Permanent Collection, The Museum of Modern Art, New York, Acquired through the Lillie P. Bliss Bequest.

183

BRAQUE. The Round Table. Phillips Collection, Washington, D.C.

CHAGALL. I and the Village. Permanent Collection, The Museum of Modern Art, New York, Mrs. Simon Guggenheim Fund.

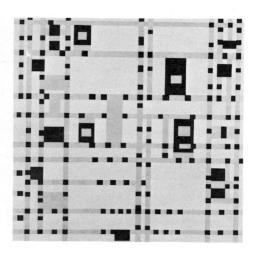

MONDRIAN. Broadway Boogie Woogie. Permanent Collection, The Museum of Modern Art, New York.

Michelangelo, mighty painter, poet, sculptor, architect, man of unceasing energy and fiery temperament, at war with the world and himself, who never knew peace.

Raphael, who with elegance and dignity transposed the trials and the efforts of two hundred years into the perfect order and harmony of the High Renaissance.

We have seen the luminous beauty of *Venice,* queen of the waters, the poetry of *Giorgione's* idyllic landscapes, the flesh tones of *Titian's* pagan women, the light of the sky, the love of color for itself.

The practical merchant world of the north—from the *van Eycks* with their incomparable ability to paint small pictures and fine details to the sweeping grandeur of *Rubens.*

The Baroque world of space and movement, ennobled by *Velásquez's* cool, unimpassioned painter's eye, and shattered by *El Greco's* frenzied distortions.

The deep moral beauty of an old man's head painted by *Rembrandt,* who stood alone.

There was a time of grayness, when dictators and academies and poor taste reigned, when for 150 years the life of the painter was a constant fight for freedom, when the rebels *Delacroix, Courbet, Daumier* stood firm.

And art's final release into the sunshine and aliveness of Impressionism—the years of striving and sacrifice that cost many painters their lives but gave our century a new art, the great rainbow that reached from *Manet* to *Cézanne.*

On the walls of the museums and galleries of the world hang pictures from all these centuries. Some of these pictures the gallery-walker likes, others he dislikes. But the final judgment as to which picture is truly great rests not on how many people like it, but on the personality of the artist who painted it. No way of painting is superior or inferior to another. It is a matter of whether or not the style expresses the painter. Old masters portrayed madonnas. The moderns portray apples. No matter what the period of time, no matter what the beauty or ugliness of his model, regardless of technique, the value of the painter's creation depends on the worthiness of his ideal, and the degree to which he has made that ideal clear in his finished picture. In today's art we may not always understand what the artist is saying, or recognize the object he is painting, but we sometimes can feel the urgent desire which prompted him, and we must look in his picture for its fulfillment. As a wise man Venturi said, "We must look with the eyes of the mind into the painter's soul."

NOTE ON MUSEUMS AND GALLERIES

Throughout the United States there are many outstanding museums and galleries where the originals of great works of art are exhibited. Of course, many limit their collections to specialized fields, such as the works of American painters or modern art. The following is a list of some museums and galleries in the United States which exhibit various periods of art.

CALIFORNIA

Los Angeles County Museum
Exposition Park
Los Angeles, California

Fine Arts Society of San Diego
Balboa Park, P. O. Box 2107
San Diego, California

California Palace of the Legion of Honor
Lincoln Park
San Francisco, California

M. H. De Young Memorial Museum
Golden Gate Park
San Francisco, California

Henry E. Huntington Library and Art Gallery
San Marino, California

CONNECTICUT

Wadsworth Atheneum
25 Atheneum Square North
Hartford, Connecticut

DISTRICT OF COLUMBIA

The Corcoran Gallery of Art
17th Street and New York Avenue, N.W.
Washington, D. C.

National Collection of Fine Arts
Constitution Avenue at 10th Street, N.W.
Washington, D. C.

The National Gallery of Art
Constitution Avenue at 6th Street, N.W.
Washington, D. C.

The Phillips Collection
1600 21st Street, N.W.
Washington, D. C.

FLORIDA

The John and Mabel Ringling Museum of Art
Sarasota, Florida

Norton Gallery and School of Art
West Palm Beach, Florida

GEORGIA

Atlanta Art Association Galleries
1280 Peachtree Street, N.E.
Atlanta, Georgia

ILLINOIS

Art Institute of Chicago
Michigan Avenue at Adams Street
Chicago, Illinois

INDIANA

Art Association of Indianapolis,
Herron Museum of Art
110 East 16th Street
Indianapolis, Indiana

IOWA

Des Moines Art Center
Greenwood Park
Des Moines, Iowa

MARYLAND

The Baltimore Museum of Art
Wyman Park
Baltimore, Maryland

The Walters Art Gallery
600 North Charles Street
Baltimore, Maryland

MASSACHUSETTS

The Isabella Stewart Gardner Museum
280 The Fenway
Boston, Massachusetts

The Museum of Fine Arts
Huntington Avenue
Boston, Massachusetts

William Hayes Fogg Art Museum
Harvard University
Quincy Street and Broadway
Cambridge, Massachusetts

Sterling and Francine
Clark Art Institute
South Street
Williamstown, Massachusetts

Worcester Art Museum
55 Salisbury Street at Tuckerman Street
Worcester, Massachusetts

MICHIGAN

Detroit Institute of Arts
5200 Woodward Avenue
Detroit, Michigan

MINNESOTA

The Minneapolis Institute of Arts
201 East 24th Street
Minneapolis, Minnesota

MISSOURI

The William Rockhill
Nelson Gallery of Art
4525 Oak Street
Kansas City, Missouri

The City Art Museum of St. Louis
Forest Park
St. Louis, Missouri

NEBRASKA

The Joslyn Art Museum
2218 Dodge Street
Omaha, Nebraska

NEW YORK

Albright-Knox Art Gallery
1285 Elmwood Avenue
Buffalo, New York

The Frick Collection
1 East 70th Street
New York, New York

The Metropolitan Museum of Art
Fifth Avenue and 82nd Street
New York City, New York

The Museum of Modern Art
11 West 53rd Street
New York City, New York

NORTH CAROLINA

Mint Museum of Art
501 Hempstead Place
Charlotte, North Carolina

The North Carolina Museum
of Art
107 East Morgan Street
Raleigh, North Carolina

OHIO

The Cincinnati Art Museum
Eden Park
Cincinnati, Ohio

The Cleveland Museum of Art
11150 East Boulevard
Cleveland, Ohio

Columbus Gallery of Fine Arts
480 East Broad Street
Columbus, Ohio

The Toledo Museum of Art
Box 1013
Toledo, Ohio

OREGON

Portland Art Museum
South West Park and
Madison Street
Portland, Oregon

PENNSYLVANIA

The Philadelphia Museum of Art
Parkway at Fairmount Avenue
Philadelphia, Pennsylvania

Museum of Art
Carnegie Institute
4400 Forbes Avenue
Pittsburgh, Pennsylvania

RHODE ISLAND

Museum of Art,
Rhode Island School of Design
224 Benefit Street
Providence, Rhode Island

TEXAS

The Museum of Fine Arts
of Houston
1001 Bissonet Street
Houston, Texas

VIRGINIA

The Virginia Museum of Fine Arts
Grove Avenue and The Boulevard
Richmond, Virginia

WASHINGTON

Seattle Art Museum
Volunteer Park
Seattle, Washington

On the following pages is a chart of the painters referred to in this book that indicates those museums and galleries in which you might find examples of the painter's work. Every effort has been made to make the list complete, but the contents of collections is constantly changing as new additions are acquired.

It is important to remember that the museums and galleries exhibit many more works of art than those listed in the chart; generally, information bureaus and monthly brochures will give you correct listings of both permanent and transient collections.

Museum	Bellinis, The	Blake, W.	Botticelli, S.	Brueghel, P.	Breughel, J.	Canaletto	Caravaggio	Cassatt, M.	Cézanne	Cimabue	Constable, J.	Corot, C.	Courbet, C.	Daumier, G.	David, J.L.	Da Vinci, L.	Degas, E.	De Hooch, P.	Delacroix, E.	Della Francesca	Donatello	Duccio	Dürer, A.	El Greco	Fra Angelico	Fra Filippo Lippi	Gainsborough, T.	Gauguin, P.	Ghirlandaio, D.	Giorgione	Giotto
Albright Art Gallery		✓				✓			✓		✓	✓	✓	✓		✓		✓					✓				✓	✓			
Art Association of Indianapolis				✓	✓		✓	✓			✓	✓	✓	✓		✓											✓	✓			
Art Institute of Chicago					✓		✓	✓			✓	✓	✓	✓		✓	✓						✓					✓			
Atlanta Art Association Galleries	✓	✓					✓	✓	✓		✓	✓	✓	✓											✓						
Baltimore Museum of Art		✓				✓		✓	✓		✓	✓	✓			✓		✓					✓				✓	✓			✓
California Palace of the Legion of Honor				✓					✓		✓	✓		✓		✓		✓						✓			✓				
Carnegie Institution		✓						✓			✓	✓	✓			✓						✓					✓				
Cincinnati Art Museum			✓			✓		✓	✓		✓	✓	✓	✓		✓	✓	✓					✓				✓				
City Art Museum of St. Louis		✓				✓		✓	✓		✓	✓				✓	✓	✓					✓				✓	✓			
Clark Art Institute		✓						✓			✓	✓	✓			✓				✓							✓		✓		
Cleveland Museum of Art		✓		✓		✓		✓	✓		✓	✓	✓	✓	✓	✓	✓	✓					✓	✓		✓	✓	✓			
Columbus Gallery of Fine Arts																															
Corcoran Gallery of Art	✓			✓			✓				✓	✓	✓	✓		✓		✓		✓			✓		✓			✓	✓	✓	
Des Moines Art Center											✓	✓	✓														✓				
Detroit Institute of Arts	✓		✓	✓	✓	✓	✓	✓	✓		✓	✓	✓		✓	✓	✓	✓				✓		✓	✓	✓	✓		✓	✓	
De Young Memorial Museum									✓							✓							✓	✓	✓						
Fine Arts Society of San Diego	✓				✓	✓	✓	✓	✓		✓	✓	✓	✓									✓	✓				✓	✓	✓	
Fogg Art Museum	✓	✓	✓	✓		✓		✓	✓		✓	✓	✓	✓		✓		✓					✓	✓	✓	✓	✓	✓	✓		✓
Frick Collection	✓	✓							✓	✓			✓			✓			✓		✓		✓		✓	✓	✓				
Gardner Museum	✓		✓								✓					✓			✓					✓						✓	✓
Henry E. Huntington		✓								✓															✓						
Joslyn Art Museum								✓			✓	✓	✓						✓				✓								
Los Angeles County Museum				✓	✓		✓	✓			✓	✓	✓	✓		✓	✓	✓					✓				✓	✓			
Metropolitan Museum of Art	✓	✓	✓	✓	✓	✓	✓	✓	✓		✓	✓	✓	✓	✓	✓	✓	✓		✓	✓	✓	✓	✓	✓	✓	✓	✓	✓	✓	✓
Minneapolis Institute of Arts			✓			✓			✓		✓	✓	✓	✓		✓		✓					✓				✓	✓			
Mint Museum of Art																												✓			
Museum of Art, Rhode Island School of Design		✓		✓	✓		✓	✓			✓	✓	✓	✓		✓		✓				✓	✓		✓						
Museum of Fine Arts of Boston	✓	✓		✓	✓		✓	✓	✓	✓		✓	✓	✓	✓	✓		✓	✓		✓	✓	✓	✓	✓	✓	✓	✓			
Museum of Fine Arts of Houston									✓														✓								
Museum of Modern Art									✓				✓			✓									✓						
National Collection of Fine Arts																							✓								
National Gallery of Art	✓	✓	✓		✓		✓	✓	✓	✓	✓	✓	✓	✓	✓	✓		✓	✓	✓	✓	✓	✓	✓	✓	✓	✓	✓	✓	✓	✓
Nelson Gallery of Art	✓			✓		✓	✓		✓		✓	✓	✓	✓	✓								✓				✓	✓			
North Carolina Museum of Art				✓										✓											✓						
Norton Gallery and School of Art								✓																	✓						
Philadelphia Museum of Art	✓	✓	✓	✓	✓	✓		✓	✓		✓	✓	✓	✓		✓	✓	✓			✓		✓	✓	✓		✓	✓	✓		
Phillips Collection								✓			✓	✓	✓	✓		✓		✓					✓				✓		✓		
Portland Art Museum	✓		✓								✓	✓				✓		✓									✓				
Ringling Museum of Art					✓																		✓		✓						
Seattle Art Museum			✓		✓		✓						✓					✓				✓	✓		✓		✓				
Toledo Museum of Art													✓										✓								
Virginia Museum of Fine Arts																	✓								✓						
Wadsworth Atheneum				✓	✓	✓	✓	✓	✓		✓	✓	✓	✓	✓	✓		✓					✓	✓	✓		✓	✓			
Walters Art Gallery	✓			✓	✓		✓				✓	✓	✓			✓		✓					✓		✓						
Worcester Art Museum																							✓		✓						

INDEX

ABOUT THE AUTHOR

Born and brought up in Massachusetts, BERNARDINE KIELTY now lives in New York City. She is married to Harry Scherman, author and publisher, and is the mother of two children, one a musician, the other a writer. For several years she was book columnist for *The Ladies Home Journal,* wrote three historical biographies for teen-agers, and edited the perennially popular *A Treasury of Short Stories.* Her most recent book, GIRL FROM FITCHBURG, reflects the impact of New York on a dyed-in-the-wool New Englander.

Bernardine Kielty's love of art is long-standing as well as enthusiastic, and has taken her to the great and small museums of Europe and America. The result is this book, MASTERS OF PAINTING, which expresses her own lively and informed interest in her subject.